EDITOR: Maryanne Blacker

FOOD EDITOR: Pamela Clark

■ ■ ■

ART DIRECTOR: Robbylee Phelan

■ ■ ■

ASSISTANT FOOD EDITORS: Kathy Snowball, Louise Patniotis

ASSOCIATE FOOD EDITOR: Enid Morrison

SENIOR HOME ECONOMISTS: Kathy McGarry, Sophia Young

HOME ECONOMISTS: Cynthia Black, Leisel Chen, Bronwen Clark, Caroline Jones

EDITORIAL COORDINATOR: Elizabeth Hooper

KITCHEN ASSISTANT: Amy Wong

■ ■ ■

STYLISTS: Wendy Berecry, Lucy Andrews, Marie-Helene Clauzon, Carolyn Fienberg, Jane Hann, Rosemary de Santis

PHOTOGRAPHERS: Kevin Brown, Robert Clark, Robert Taylor, Jon Waddy

■ ■ ■

HOME LIBRARY STAFF:

ART DIRECTOR: Sue de Guingand

ASSISTANT EDITOR: Bridget van Tinteren

EDITORIAL COORDINATOR: Fiona Lambrou

■ ■ ■

ACP PUBLISHER: Richard Walsh

ACP DEPUTY PUBLISHER: Nick Chan

ACP CIRCULATION & MARKETING DIRECTOR: Judy Kiernan

■ ■ ■

Produced by The Australian Women's Weekly Home Library. Typeset by ACP Colour Graphics Pty. Ltd. Colour separations by Network Graphics Pty. Ltd., Sydney. Printed by Times Printers Pte. Ltd., Singapore. Published by ACP Publishing Pty. Limited, 54 Park Street, Sydney.
♦ **AUSTRALIA:** Distributed by Network Distribution Company, 54 Park Street Sydney, (02) 282 8777.
♦ **UNITED KINGDOM:** Distributed in the U.K. by Australian Consolidated Press (UK) Ltd, 20 Galowhill Rd, Brackmills, Northampton NN4 7EE (01604) 760 456.
♦ **CANADA:** Distributed in Canada by WhitecapBooks Ltd, 351 Lynn Ave, Vancouver B.C. V7J 2C4 (604) 980 9852.
♦ **NEW ZEALAND:** Distributed in New Zealand by Netlink Distribution Company, 17B Hargreaves St, Level 5, College Hill, Auckland 1 (9) 302 7616.
♦ **SOUTH AFRICA:** Distributed in South Africa by Intermag, PO Box 57394, Springfield 2137 (011) 493 3200.

■ ■ ■

Saucery

Includes index.
ISBN 1 86396 018 X

1. Sauces. 2. Cookery (Salad dressing).
(Series: Australian Women's Weekly Home Library)

641.814

■ ■ ■

■ ■ ■

COVER: Clockwise from front right: Pesto, page 10, Nutty Red and Yellow Pepper Sauce, page 96, Strawberry Sauce, page 113, Passionfruit Sauce, page 113, Seafood Cocktail Sauce, page 40, Mushroom and Port Sauce, page 20 *China, sauce boat, ladle from Royal Copenhagen; glass jugs, mortar and pestle from Accoutrement.*
OPPOSITE: Clockwise from top: Blueberry Butter Sauce, Melba Sauce, page 115, Mango and Lime Sauce, page 115, Tropical Fruit Sauce, page 114.
BACK COVER: From top: Tamarillo Sauce, Prosciutto and Tomato Sauce, page 26.

SAUCERY

With our inspirational sauces, you have meal-making magic for every occasion. There are endless ideas for transforming seafood, chicken, meat, vegies and more into feasts of flavour. Desserts can be especially glamorous with a saucy addition, and now you'll find it so easy to dress up ice-cream, fruit, cakes and pastries. One taste, and you'll be spellbound.

Pamela Clark

FOOD EDITOR

BRITISH & NORTH AMERICAN READERS: Please note that Australian cup and spoon measurements are metric. A quick conversion guide appears on page 127.
A glossary explaining unfamiliar terms and ingredients appears on page 122.

for pasta

When serving these sauces, allow up to 125g uncooked pasta per person. Many of these sauces can be used over ingredients other than pasta.

CURRIED CREAM SAUCE

30g butter
3 teaspoons mild curry powder
2 green shallots, chopped
½ teaspoon ground cumin
1 small fresh red chilli, chopped
340ml can coconut milk
2 tablespoons chopped fresh chives
2 tablespoons chopped
    fresh coriander

Heat butter in pan, add curry powder, shallots, cumin and chilli, cook, stirring, until fragrant. Stir in coconut milk, simmer, uncovered, about 5 minutes or until sauce thickens slightly; stir in herbs.

Serves 4. Makes about 1¼ cups (310ml).

■ Sauce best made just before serving.
■ Freeze: Not suitable.
■ Microwave: Suitable.
Also suitable for: Chicken, fish.

SALAMI AND CHILLI SAUCE

200g butter
6 green shallots, chopped
3 cloves garlic, crushed
2 medium fresh red chillies, seeded,
    finely chopped
200g piece salami, chopped
1 cup (80g) grated parmesan cheese
¼ cup chopped fresh parsley
¼ cup chopped fresh basil

Heat butter in pan, add shallots, garlic, chilli and salami, cook, stirring, until shallots are soft. Remove from heat, stir in cheese and herbs.

Serves 4. Makes about 2 cups (500ml).

■ Recipe best made just before serving.
■ Freeze: Not suitable.
■ Microwave: Suitable.
Also suitable for: Rice.

RIGHT: From left: Curried Cream Sauce, Salami and Chilli Sauce.

MARINARA SAUCE

250g calamari tubes
750g small mussels
2 x 410g cans tomatoes
1 tablespoon olive oil
2 cloves garlic, crushed
1 tablespoon tomato paste
1/4 cup (60ml) dry white wine
500g cooked prawns, shelled
1/3 cup chopped fresh parsley

Cut calamari open, score criss-cross pattern on inside, cut into 3cm-wide strips. Drop calamari into pan of boiling water, return to boil; drain immediately.

Scrub mussels, remove beards. Place mussels in large pan, cover with water, cook, covered, over high heat about 3 minutes or until mussels open; drain. Remove mussels from shells; discard shells. Blend or process undrained tomatoes until smooth.

Heat oil and garlic in pan, add pureed tomatoes, tomato paste and wine, simmer, uncovered, about 20 minutes or until sauce is thick. Stir in seafood and parsley, stir until heated through.

Serves 4.

▨ Recipe best made close to serving.
▨ Freeze: Not suitable.
▨ Microwave: Not suitable.

CARBONARA SAUCE

500g spaghetti
1 tablespoon olive oil
5 bacon rashers, sliced
1/2 cup (125ml) dry white wine
1/2 cup (125ml) cream
4 egg yolks
1/2 cup (40g) grated parmesan cheese
2 tablespoons chopped fresh parsley

Add pasta to large pan of boiling water, simmer, uncovered, until tender, drain. Heat oil in pan, add bacon, cook, stirring, until crisp. Stir in wine and cream, bring to boil; remove from heat. Toss hot pasta with bacon mixture, add combined egg yolks, cheese and parsley; mix gently.

Serves 4.

▨ Recipe best made close to serving.
▨ Freeze: Not suitable.
▨ Microwave: Suitable.

ABOVE: From left: Carbonara Sauce, Marinara Sauce.
RIGHT: From left: Peanut Sauce, Spinach Beetroot Sauce.

Above: Tiles from Country Floors. Right: Plates and bowl from Accoutrement; tiles from Country Floors.

SPINACH BEETROOT SAUCE

2 bunches (about 20) baby beetroot
2 tablespoons olive oil
1 medium (350g) leek, sliced
1 clove garlic, crushed
1 bunch (about 650g) English
  spinach, shredded
2/3 cup (160ml) dry white wine
300ml cream
125g packet cream cheese, chopped
2/3 cup (50g) grated parmesan cheese
1 tablespoon chopped fresh oregano
1 small chicken stock cube

Trim leaves from beetroot, reserve about 10 leaves; shred leaves. Boil, steam or microwave unpeeled beetroot until tender; peel away skin.

Heat oil in pan, add leek and garlic, cook, stirring, until leek is soft. Add beetroot leaves and spinach leaves, cook, stirring, until wilted. Add wine, bring to boil, stir in cream, cheeses, oregano and crumbled stock cube, simmer, uncovered, until cheese is melted and sauce thickened slightly. Just before serving, stir in beetroot.

Serves 4.

▨ Recipe best made close to serving.
▨ Freeze: Not suitable.
▨ Microwave: Beetroot suitable.
Also suitable for: Rice.

PEANUT SAUCE

1⅓ cups (200g) shelled
  unroasted peanuts
¾ cup (180ml) warm black tea
3 cloves garlic, crushed
1 tablespoon grated fresh ginger
1 teaspoon sambal oelek
½ cup (125ml) peanut oil
1 tablespoon soy sauce
1½ tablespoons white vinegar
2 teaspoons sesame oil
2 teaspoons sugar
1 tablespoon chopped
  fresh coriander

Place peanuts on oven tray, bake in moderate oven about 5 minutes or until lightly browned; cool. Process peanuts until coarsely chopped. Add ¼ cup (60ml) of the tea, garlic, ginger and sambal oelek, process until combined. Add peanut oil in a thin stream while motor is operating. Add remaining tea, soy sauce, vinegar, sesame oil and sugar, process until combined; stir in coriander.

Serves 4. Makes about 2 cups (500ml).

■ Recipe can be made a day ahead.
■ Storage: Covered, in refrigerator.
■ Freeze: Not suitable.
■ Microwave: Not suitable.
Also suitable for: Vegetables, chicken, beef, pork.

TOMATO AND BLACK BEAN SAUCE

2 tablespoons olive oil
3 small fresh red chillies, seeded, chopped
3 cloves garlic, crushed
1/3 cup (35g) drained sliced sun-dried tomatoes
4 green shallots, chopped
2 tablespoons chopped fresh basil
2 teaspoons grated fresh ginger
1/3 cup (80ml) canned black beans, rinsed, drained
410g can tomatoes
1/4 cup (60ml) tomato paste
2/3 cup (160ml) water

Heat oil in pan, add chillies, garlic, sun-dried tomatoes, shallots, basil, ginger and beans, cook, stirring, 1 minute. Blend or process undrained canned tomatoes until pureed. Add puree, paste and water to pan, stir until heated through.

Serves 4. Makes about 2 cups (500ml).

■ Sauce can be made a day ahead.
■ Storage: Covered, in refrigerator.
■ Freeze: Not suitable.
■ Microwave: Suitable.

Also suitable for: Beef, tuna.

ARTICHOKE, PEPPER AND HAM SAUCE

2 medium (400g) red peppers
200g sliced ham
1/2 cup (125ml) olive oil
2 cloves garlic, crushed
6 green shallots, chopped
8 artichoke hearts in oil, drained, halved
2 tablespoons chopped fresh flat-leafed parsley
1 cup (80g) parmesan cheese flakes

Quarter peppers, remove seeds and membrane. Grill peppers, skin side up, until skin blisters and blackens. Peel away skin, cut peppers into thin strips.

Cut ham into thin strips. Heat oil in pan, add garlic and shallots, cook, stirring, until shallots are soft. Add peppers, ham and artichokes, stir over heat until heated through; stir in parsley. Top with cheese.

Serves 4. Makes about 1 litre (4 cups).

■ Sauce can be made several hours ahead.
■ Storage: Covered, in refrigerator.
■ Freeze: Not suitable.
■ Microwave: Not suitable.

Also suitable for: Rice.

BUTTER BEAN AND SPINACH SAUCE

1 cup (250ml) olive oil
1 medium (300g) red Spanish onion, sliced
2 cloves garlic, crushed
1 bunch (about 650g) English spinach, shredded
2 teaspoons grated lemon rind
1/4 cup (60ml) lemon juice
3 medium tomatoes, peeled, seeded, chopped
310g can butter beans, rinsed, drained
2 tablespoons chopped fresh parsley
2 tablespoons chopped fresh mint

Heat 1/4 cup (60ml) of the oil in pan, add onion and garlic, cook, stirring, until onion is soft. Add spinach, stir over heat until just wilted. Add remaining oil, rind, juice, tomatoes and beans; stir until heated through, stir in herbs.

Serves 4. Makes about 2 cups (500ml).

■ Sauce can be made a day ahead.
■ Storage: Covered, in refrigerator.
■ Freeze: Not suitable.
■ Microwave: Suitable.

Also suitable for: Tuna.

CORIANDER AND PECAN PESTO

1/2 cup chopped fresh coriander
1 tablespoon chopped coriander roots and stems
1/3 cup firmly packed fresh basil leaves
2 cloves garlic, crushed
1 tablespoon pine nuts, toasted
1/3 cup (60g) chopped pecans, toasted
2 tablespoons grated parmesan cheese
1/2 cup (125ml) olive oil

Process coriander, roots and stems, basil, garlic, nuts and cheese until smooth. Add oil in a thin stream while motor is operating; process mixture until smooth.

Serves 4. Makes about 1 cup (250ml).

■ Pesto can be made a day ahead.
■ Storage: Covered with plastic wrap on surface, in refrigerator.
■ Freeze: Suitable.

Also suitable for: Lamb, chicken, fish, vegetables.

LEFT: From top: Tomato and Black Bean Sauce, Artichoke, Pepper and Ham Sauce.
RIGHT: From left: Butter Bean and Spinach Sauce, Coriander and Pecan Pesto.

CREAMY MUSHROOM AND PASTRAMI SAUCE

1 medium (200g) red pepper
125g sliced pastrami
20g butter
1 tablespoon light olive oil
2 cloves garlic, crushed
3 green shallots, chopped
250g button mushrooms, sliced
300ml sour cream
¼ cup (60ml) cream
1 tablespoon chopped fresh chives

Quarter pepper, remove seeds and membrane. Grill pepper, skin side up, until skin blisters and blackens. Peel away skin, cut pepper into thin strips. Cut pastrami into thin strips.

Heat butter and oil in pan, add garlic, shallots and mushrooms, cook, stirring, 2 minutes. Add creams, simmer, uncovered, until thickened slightly. Add pepper, pastrami and chives; stir until hot.

Serves 8. Makes about 1 litre (4 cups).

■ Sauce best made just before serving.
■ Freeze: Not suitable.
■ Microwave: Suitable.

CAPER AND ROASTED PEPPER SALSA

1 medium (200g) red pepper
1 medium (200g) green pepper
1 medium (200g) yellow pepper
3 medium (390g) tomatoes, peeled, seeded, sliced
1 small (100g) red Spanish onion, thinly sliced
¼ cup (60ml) drained baby capers
¼ cup shredded fresh basil
2 tablespoons balsamic vinegar
½ cup (125ml) virgin olive oil
3 teaspoons black olive paste
2 cloves garlic, crushed

Quarter peppers, remove seeds and membrane. Grill peppers, skin side up, until skin blisters and blackens. Peel away skin, slice peppers thinly.

Combine peppers, tomatoes, onion, capers and basil in bowl, add combined vinegar, oil, paste and garlic; mix well.

Serves 4 to 6. Makes about 2 cups (500ml).

■ Salsa can be made a day ahead.
■ Storage: Covered, in refrigerator.
■ Freeze: Not suitable.
■ Microwave: Not suitable.

Also suitable for: Lamb, beef, seafood.

TOMATO AND CHICKPEA SAUCE

2 tablespoons vegetable oil
3 cloves garlic, crushed
410g can tomatoes
⅔ cup (160ml) tomato puree
½ cup (125ml) water
1 teaspoon sugar
1 tablespoon chopped fresh oregano
2 teaspoons chopped fresh thyme
310g can chickpeas, rinsed, drained
¼ cup (40g) seedless black olives, sliced

Heat oil in pan, add garlic, undrained crushed tomatoes, puree, water, sugar and herbs, simmer, uncovered, until sauce is thickened slightly. Add chickpeas and olives, stir over heat until hot.

Serves 4. Makes about 1 litre (4 cups).

■ Sauce can be made a day ahead.
■ Storage: Covered, in refrigerator.
■ Freeze: Suitable.
■ Microwave: Suitable.

Also suitable for: Lamb.

RADICCHIO AND ROCKET CREAM

2 medium (700g) leeks
60g butter
3 cloves garlic, crushed
½ cup (125ml) dry white wine
1 cup (250ml) vegetable stock
2 radicchio lettuce, shredded
2 bunches (about 240g) rocket
300ml cream
⅓ cup shredded fresh basil
½ teaspoon sugar

Cut leeks into very thin strips lengthways. Heat butter in pan, add leeks and garlic, cook, stirring, until leeks are soft. Add wine and stock, simmer, uncovered, until reduced by half. Stir in radicchio, rocket, cream, basil and sugar, simmer, uncovered, until radicchio and rocket are just wilted and sauce is hot.

Serves 4. Makes about 1 litre (4 cups).

■ Recipe best made close to serving.
■ Freeze: Not suitable.
■ Microwave: Suitable.

TUNA AND PEPPER SAUCE

3 medium (600g) red peppers
2 tablespoons olive oil
1 medium (150g) onion, finely chopped
2 cloves garlic, crushed
410g can tomatoes
½ teaspoon sugar
2 x 185g cans tuna, drained, flaked
¼ cup shredded fresh basil

Quarter peppers, remove seeds and membrane. Grill peppers, skin side up, until skin blisters and blackens. Peel away skin.

Heat oil in pan, add onion and garlic, cook, stirring, until onion is soft. Blend or process peppers, onion mixture, undrained crushed tomatoes and sugar until smooth. Return mixture to pan, add tuna and basil; stir until heated through.

Serves 4. Makes about 2 cups (500ml).

■ Sauce can be made a day ahead.
■ Storage: Covered, in refrigerator.
■ Freeze: Not suitable.
■ Microwave: Suitable.
Also suitable for: Veal.

LEFT: Clockwise from left: Creamy Mushroom and Pastrami Sauce, Caper and Roasted Pepper Salsa, Tomato and Chickpea Sauce. ABOVE: Clockwise from left: Tuna and Pepper Sauce, Radicchio and Rocket Cream, Creamy Seafood Sauce.

Above: Saucepans and ladle from The Bay Tree Kitchen Shop.

CREAMY SEAFOOD SAUCE

500g uncooked king prawns
250g firm white fish fillets
60g smoked salmon
30g butter
1 medium (150g) onion, finely chopped
¼ cup (60ml) dry white wine
2 tablespoons water
125g scallops
½ cup (125ml) sour cream
2 tablespoons cream
2 teaspoons seeded mustard

Shell and devein prawns leaving tails intact. Cut fish into 2cm pieces. Cut salmon into thin strips.

Heat butter in pan, add onion, cook, stirring, until soft. Add wine and water, bring to boil, add prawns, fish and scallops, simmer, uncovered, until seafood is just tender. Remove seafood from pan; drain on absorbent paper. Reheat sauce, boil, uncovered, until reduced to ¼ cup (60ml). Add creams, simmer, uncovered, 3 minutes. Remove pan from heat, stir in all seafood and mustard.

Serves 4. Makes about 1 litre (4 cups).

■ Recipe best made just before serving.
■ Freeze: Not suitable.
■ Microwave: Not suitable.

VEGETABLE AND SWEET CHILLI SAUCE

2 medium (250g) carrots
2 sticks celery
1 medium leek
1 medium (200g) red pepper
1 medium (200g) yellow pepper
1 tablespoon light olive oil
1 tablespoon grated fresh ginger
2 cloves garlic, crushed
30g snow pea sprouts
1/4 cup (60ml) lime juice
2 1/2 tablespoons mild sweet chilli sauce
2 teaspoons sesame oil
1 tablespoon fish sauce
1/2 cup (125ml) light olive oil, extra
3 teaspoons brown sugar
1/4 cup chopped fresh coriander

Cut carrots, celery, leek and peppers into thin strips. Heat oil in pan, add leek, ginger and garlic, cook, stirring, until leek is soft. Add carrots, celery and peppers, cook, stirring, until vegetables are just tender. Add remaining ingredients, stir until heated through.

Serves 4.

■ Recipe best made just before serving.
■ Freeze: Not suitable.
■ Microwave: Not suitable.
Also suitable for: Beef, pork.

PESTO

2 cups firmly packed fresh basil leaves
1/2 cup (80g) pine nuts, toasted
2 cloves garlic, crushed
1/2 cup (125ml) olive oil
1/3 cup (25g) grated parmesan cheese

Process basil, nuts and garlic until finely chopped. Add oil in a thin stream while motor is operating, process until combined. Add cheese, process mixture until well combined.

Serves 4. Makes about 1 1/4 cups (310ml).

■ Recipe can be made a day ahead.
■ Storage: Covered with plastic wrap on surface, in refrigerator.
■ Freeze: Suitable.
Also suitable for: Seafood, chicken, lamb, vegetables.

CURRANT AND PINE NUT SAUCE

2 tablespoons olive oil
2 bacon rashers, chopped
2 medium (300g) onions, finely chopped
2 cloves garlic, crushed
1/4 teaspoon ground cinnamon
2 teaspoons ground cumin
2 teaspoons ground coriander
1 teaspoon garam masala
3 medium (390g) tomatoes, chopped
1 cup (250ml) water
1/3 cup (50g) dried currants
1/3 cup (50g) pine nuts
1/4 cup shredded fresh basil

Heat oil in pan, add bacon, cook, stirring, until browned and crisp. Add onions and garlic, cook, stirring, until onions are soft. Add spices, cook, stirring, until fragrant. Add tomatoes, water and currants, cook, uncovered, about 5 minutes or until sauce is slightly thickened. Just before serving, stir in nuts and basil.

Serves 4. Makes about 3 1/2 cups (875ml).

■ Sauce can be made a day ahead.
■ Freeze: Suitable.
■ Microwave: Suitable.
Also suitable for: Lamb, chicken.

CREAMY HERB AND CHICKEN SAUCE

2 single chicken breast fillets
1 cup (250ml) chicken stock
1 tablespoon cornflour
¼ cup (60ml) dry white wine
300ml cream
¾ cup (60g) grated parmesan cheese
3 green shallots, chopped
1 tablespoon chopped fresh parsley
1 tablespoon chopped fresh oregano
1 tablespoon chopped fresh chives

Place chicken and stock in pan, simmer, covered, until chicken is just tender; cool chicken in stock. Remove chicken from stock, strain and reserve stock. Shred chicken finely.

Combine blended cornflour and wine with cream, cheese and reserved stock in pan, stir over heat until mixture boils and thickens; stir in chicken, shallots and herbs.

Serves 4. Makes about 2 cups (500ml).

- Sauce can be made a day ahead.
- Storage: Covered, in refrigerator.
- Freeze: Not suitable.
- Microwave: Suitable.

LEFT: From left: Pesto, Vegetable and Sweet Chilli Sauce.
BELOW: From top: Creamy Herb and Chicken Sauce, Currant and Pine Nut Sauce.

Left: Mortar and pestle from The Bay Tree Kitchen Shop. Below: Serving ware from Hale Imports

VONGOLE SAUCE

2 medium (300g) onions,
    finely chopped
3 cloves garlic, chopped
½ cup (125ml) dry white wine
1 cup (250ml) chicken stock
1½ tablespoons cornflour
1kg small fresh clams
⅓ cup chopped fresh
    flat-leafed parsley

Combine onions, garlic and wine in pan, simmer, uncovered, about 5 minutes or until reduced by half. Stir in blended chicken stock and cornflour, stir until mixture boils and thickens. Add clams, simmer, covered, about 3 minutes or until clams open; stir in parsley.

Serves 4.

 ▪ Recipe best made close to serving.
 ▪ Freeze: Not suitable.
 ▪ Microwave: Not suitable.

CORIANDER, LIME AND GINGER BUTTER

250g butter, chopped
2 teaspoons grated fresh ginger
2 tablespoons lime juice
¼ cup chopped fresh coriander

CRISP BREADCRUMBS
2 tablespoons light olive oil
1½ cups (110g) stale breadcrumbs

Combine butter, ginger and juice in pan, stir over heat until butter is just melted, do not boil; stir in coriander. Pour butter sauce over pasta, sprinkle with crisp breadcrumbs.

Crisp Breadcrumbs: Heat oil in pan, add breadcrumbs, stir over heat until browned and crisp.

Serves 4 to 6. Makes 1¼ cups (310ml).

 ▪ Sauce best made close to serving.
 ▪ Freeze: Not suitable.
 ▪ Microwave: Sauce suitable.

PEA AND PROSCIUTTO SAUCE

60g butter
2 tablespoons olive oil
2 cloves garlic, crushed
3 large (900g) red Spanish
    onions, sliced
2 cups (250g) frozen peas, thawed
7 slices prosciutto, chopped
¼ cup (35g) drained chopped
    sun-dried tomatoes

Heat butter and oil in pan, add garlic and onions, cook, covered, stirring occasionally, until onions are very soft. Add peas, prosciutto and tomatoes, stir until heated through.

Serves 4. Makes about 3 cups (750ml).

 ▪ Recipe best made close to serving.
 ▪ Freeze: Not suitable.
 ▪ Microwave: Not suitable.

Also suitable for: Veal.

EGGPLANT, OLIVE AND ANCHOVY SAUCE

⅓ cup (80ml) light olive oil
1 small (230g) eggplant, chopped
1 medium (150g) onion, finely chopped
2 cloves garlic, crushed
1 medium (200g) green pepper,
    finely chopped
2 x 425g cans tomatoes
¾ cup (180ml) chicken stock
½ teaspoon sugar
¼ cup chopped fresh basil
½ x 45g can anchovy fillets,
    drained, chopped
10 seedless black olives,
    finely chopped
1 tablespoon drained capers,
    chopped
¼ cup chopped fresh parsley

Heat oil in pan, add eggplant, onion, garlic and pepper, cook, stirring, until onion and eggplant are just soft. Add undrained crushed tomatoes, stock, sugar and basil, simmer, covered, about 30 minutes, or until slightly thickened. Add remaining ingredients; stir until heated through.

Serves 4. Makes about 1.25 litres
(5 cups).

 ▪ Recipe can be made a day ahead.
 ▪ Storage: Covered, in refrigerator.
 ▪ Freeze: Suitable.
 ▪ Microwave: Not suitable.

Also suitable for: Lamb, chicken, pork.

CREAMY KUMARA SAUCE

2 small (about 500g) kumara, peeled
2 tablespoons olive oil
1 clove garlic, crushed
300ml cream
½ cup (125ml) dry white wine
⅓ cup (25g) grated parmesan cheese
2 teaspoons Dijon mustard
2 tablespoons chopped fresh chives

Cut 1 kumara into 1cm pieces. Boil, steam or microwave kumara until tender, drain. Coarsely grate remaining kumara.

Heat oil in pan, add grated kumara and garlic, cook, stirring, until kumara is soft. Stir in cream, wine, cheese and mustard, simmer, uncovered, about 3 minutes or until slightly thickened; stir in chopped kumara and chives.

Serves 4. Makes about 3 cups (750ml).

 ▪ Sauce can be made a day ahead.
 ▪ Storage: Covered, in refrigerator.
 ▪ Freeze: Not suitable.
 ▪ Microwave: Suitable.

ABOVE: From left: Eggplant, Olive and Anchovy Sauce, Creamy Kumara Sauce. RIGHT: Clockwise from left: Coriander, Lime and Ginger Butter, Vongole Sauce, Pea and Prosciutto Sauce.

Right and above: China from Hale Imports.

BOLOGNESE SAUCE

2 tablespoons olive oil
2 medium onions (300g),
    finely chopped
1 stick celery, chopped
2 cloves garlic, crushed
750g minced beef
2 x 410g cans tomatoes
¼ cup (60ml) tomato paste
1 teaspoon dried oregano leaves
½ teaspoon dried marjoram leaves
3 teaspoons beef stock powder
1 cup (250ml) water
½ cup (125ml) dry white wine
¼ cup shredded fresh basil

Heat oil in pan, add onions, celery and garlic, cook, stirring, until onions are very soft. Add mince, cook, stirring, until changed in colour. Stir in undrained crushed tomatoes, paste, oregano, marjoram, stock powder, water and wine. Simmer gently, uncovered, about 1½ hours or until thick; stir in basil.

Serves 6. Makes about 1.25 litres (5 cups).

■ Sauce can be made a day ahead.
■ Storage: Covered, in refrigerator.
■ Freeze: Suitable.
■ Microwave: Suitable.

ABOVE: From back: Bolognese Sauce, Creamy Asparagus Sauce.
RIGHT: From left: Red Pepper and Chilli Sauce, Bacon and Basil Sauce.

Above: Bowls from Hale Imports; saucepan from The Cottage Manner.

CREAMY ASPARAGUS SAUCE

2 bunches (about 500g) fresh
   asparagus
1 medium (170g) red Spanish onion
200g snow peas
1 tablespoon light olive oil
½ cup (65g) drained sliced
   sun-dried tomatoes
300ml sour cream
½ cup (125ml) cream
1 tablespoon seeded mustard
1 tablespoon chopped fresh chives
⅓ cup (25g) parmesan cheese flakes

Cut asparagus into 4cm lengths. Cut onion into thin wedges. Cut snow peas in half, diagonally.

Heat oil in pan, add asparagus, onion and snow peas, cook, stirring, until onion is just soft. Add tomatoes, creams and mustard, simmer, uncovered, until slightly thickened, stir in chives. Serve topped with cheese.

Serves 4 to 6. Makes about 1 litre (4 cups).

- Recipe best made close to serving.
- Freeze: Not suitable.
- Microwave: Not suitable.

Also suitable for: Chicken.

BACON AND BASIL SAUCE

1 tablespoon olive oil
4 bacon rashers, sliced
1 clove garlic, crushed
½ cup (125ml) dry white wine
300ml cream
½ cup (125ml) milk
2 teaspoons seeded mustard
2 teaspoons French mustard
¼ cup (20g) grated parmesan cheese
1 tablespoon cornflour
1 tablespoon water
½ cup shredded fresh basil
4 green shallots, chopped

Heat oil in pan, add bacon and garlic, cook, stirring, until bacon is crisp. Add wine, bring to boil. Stir in cream, milk, mustards, cheese and blended cornflour and water, stir over heat until sauce boils and thickens slightly. Stir in basil and shallots.

Serves 4. Makes about 3 cups (750ml).

- Sauce can be made a day ahead.
- Storage: Covered, in refrigerator.
- Freeze: Not suitable.
- Microwave: Suitable.

Also suitable for: Chicken.

RED PEPPER AND CHILLI SAUCE

2 medium (400g) red peppers
¼ cup (35g) drained chopped
   sun-dried tomatoes
1 small fresh red chilli,
   seeded, chopped
2 cloves garlic, crushed
1 teaspoon chopped fresh thyme
1 tablespoon tomato paste
¼ cup (60ml) olive oil

Quarter peppers, remove seeds and membrane. Grill peppers, skin side up, until skin blisters and blackens. Peel away skin, chop peppers.

Blend or process peppers and remaining ingredients until smooth.

Serves 4. Makes 1 cup (250 ml).

- Sauce can be made a day ahead.
- Storage: Covered, in refrigerator.
- Freeze: Not suitable.
- Microwave: Not suitable

Also suitable for: Beef, tuna, octopus.

GARLIC MUSHROOM SAUCE

90g butter
4 green shallots, chopped
2 cloves garlic, sliced
360g (about 8) cup mushrooms,
sliced
¼ cup (60ml) dry white wine
1¼ cups (310ml) chicken stock
1½ teaspoons Worcestershire sauce
1 tablespoon cornflour
1 tablespoon water
2 tablespoons chopped fresh chives

Heat butter in pan, add shallots, garlic and mushrooms, cook, stirring, until mushrooms are soft. Add wine, chicken stock and sauce, bring to boil. Stir in blended cornflour and water, stir over heat until sauce boils and thickens; stir in chives.

Serves 4. Makes about 2½ cups (625ml).

- Sauce can be made a day ahead.
- Storage: Covered, in refrigerator.
- Freeze: Not suitable.
- Microwave: Suitable.

Also suitable for: Chicken, beef, pasta.

PORK AND PLUM SAUCE

1 tablespoon soy sauce
1 tablespoon hoi sin sauce
½ cup (125ml) plum sauce
½ teaspoon sesame oil
¼ cup (60ml) plum jam
½ cup (125ml) water
½ teaspoon sambal oelek
2 teaspoons cornflour
1 tablespoon dry sherry
6 green shallots, chopped
250g thinly sliced Chinese
barbecued pork

Combine sauces, oil, jam, water and sambal oelek in pan, stir in blended cornflour and sherry, stir over heat until sauce boils and thickens. Stir in shallots and pork, stir until pork is heated through.

Serves 4. Makes about 2½ cups (625ml).

- Recipe best made close to serving.
- Freeze: Not suitable.
- Microwave: Suitable.

Also suitable for: Rice.

ABOVE: From left: Garlic Mushroom Sauce, Pork and Plum Sauce.
RIGHT: From left: Teriyaki Sauce, Lentil and Corn Sauce.

Above: China from Hale Imports. Right: Bowls from Accoutrement; tiles from Country Floors.

TERIYAKI SAUCE

40g butter
2 tablespoons plain flour
1¼ cups (310ml) water
¼ cup (60ml) bottled teriyaki
    marinade
⅓ cup (80ml) green ginger wine
1 teaspoon sambal oelek
20g butter, extra
½ medium (100g) red pepper,
    thinly sliced
2 green shallots, sliced
1 tablespoon chopped fresh parsley

Melt butter in pan, stir in flour, stir over heat until bubbling. Remove from heat, gradually stir in combined water, marinade, wine, sambal oelek and extra butter. Stir over heat until sauce boils and thickens, stir in pepper and shallots, simmer, uncovered, 1 minute; stir in parsley.

Serves 4. Makes about 2 cups (500ml).

- Sauce can be made a day ahead.
- Storage: Covered, in refrigerator.
- Freeze: Not suitable.
- Microwave: Suitable.

Also suitable for: Pork, fish, chicken.

LENTIL AND CORN SAUCE

2 corn cobs
40g butter
1 medium (150g) onion,
    finely chopped
1 medium (200g) red pepper, sliced
½ cup (100g) red lentils
2 cups (500ml) chicken stock
2 tablespoons chopped fresh parsley

Cut kernels from corn. Heat butter in pan, add onion and pepper, cook, stirring, until onion is soft. Add corn, lentils and stock, simmer, covered, about 8 minutes or until lentils are just tender; stir in parsley.

Serves 4 to 6. Makes about 1 litre
(4 cups).

- Sauce can be made a day ahead.
- Storage: Covered, in refrigerator.
- Freeze: Suitable.
- Microwave: Suitable.

Also suitable for: Chicken.

SAUCES
for poultry

The more robust sauces in this section will best suit richer poultry and game birds. We include serving suggestions with recipes.

MARMALADE ORANGE GLAZE

1/3 cup (80ml) dry white wine
1 tablespoon sugar
2 tablespoons marmalade
1/2 cup (125ml) orange juice
2 teaspoons cornflour
2 teaspoons Grand Marnier
2 strips orange rind, shredded

Combine wine, sugar, marmalade and 1/4 cup (60ml) of the juice blended with the cornflour in pan, cook, stirring, until mixture boils and thickens. Stir in remaining juice, liqueur and rind; stir until heated through. Served here with quail.

Serves 4. Makes about 1 cup (250ml).

■ Recipe can be made a day ahead.
■ Storage: Covered, in refrigerator.
■ Freeze: Not suitable.
■ Microwave: Suitable.
Also suitable for: Pork.

CREAMY BRANDY SAUCE

30g butter
1/2 small (40g) onion, finely chopped
3/4 cup (180ml) chicken stock
300ml cream
1 1/2 tablespoons brandy

Heat butter in pan, add onion, cook, stirring, until soft. Add stock, simmer, uncovered, about 5 minutes or until reduced by half. Add cream, simmer, uncovered, about 5 minutes or until mixture is thickened. Remove from heat, stir in brandy. Served here with chicken breast.

Serves 4. Makes about 1 1/4 cups (310ml).

■ Sauce can be made a day ahead.
■ Storage: Covered, in refrigerator.
■ Freeze: Not suitable.
■ Microwave: Not suitable.
Also suitable for: Steak.

RIGHT: From back: Marmalade Orange Glaze, Creamy Brandy Sauce.

Copper pan and saucepan from The Bay Tree Kitchen Shop.

COCONUT AND PEANUT SAUCE

½ cup (75g) unsalted roasted
   peanuts
1 clove garlic, crushed
2 teaspoons ground cumin
1 teaspoon ground coriander
½ teaspoon sambal oelek
½ teaspoon shrimp paste
1 tablespoon soy sauce
2 teaspoons brown sugar
1 tablespoon lime juice
1 cup (250ml) coconut milk
1 tablespoon chopped
   fresh coriander

Process peanuts until finely crushed.
Combine peanuts, garlic, spices, sambal
oelek, paste, soy sauce, sugar, juice and
milk in pan, simmer, uncovered, until
slightly thickened. Stir in coriander.
Served here with chicken meatballs.

Serves 4. Makes about 1½ cups (375ml).

■ Sauce can be made a day ahead.
■ Storage: Covered, in refrigerator.
■ Freeze: Not suitable.
■ Microwave: Not suitable.
*Also suitable for: Beef, lamb,
vegetables.*

LYCHEE SAUCE

425g can lychees in light syrup
1 cup (250ml) chicken stock
1 cup (250ml) water
2 tablespoons dry sherry
2 tablespoons cornflour
2 tablespoons water, extra
1 tablespoon chopped fresh parsley

Drain syrup from lychees, reserve syrup.
Quarter lychees.

   Heat reserved syrup in pan, add stock,
water and sherry, simmer, uncovered, 5
minutes. Stir in blended cornflour and
extra water, stir over heat until sauce boils
and thickens; stir in lychees and parsley.

Serves 6. Makes about 3½ cups (875ml).

■ Sauce can be made a day ahead.
■ Storage: Covered, in refrigerator.
■ Freeze: Not suitable.
■ Microwave: Suitable.
Also suitable for: Pork, veal.

MUSHROOM AND PORT SAUCE

⅔ cup (160ml) port
1 cup (250ml) water
2 teaspoons chicken stock powder
2 green shallots, chopped
40g butter
1 clove garlic, crushed
250g button mushrooms, sliced
2 teaspoons chopped fresh basil
2 teaspoons cornflour
1 tablespoon water, extra

Combine port, water, stock powder and
shallots in pan, simmer, uncovered, about
5 minutes or until reduced by half; strain.
Heat butter in pan, add garlic and mushrooms, cook, stirring, until mushrooms are
lightly browned. Add port mixture, basil
and blended cornflour and extra water.
Stir over heat constantly until sauce boils
and thickens.

Serves 4. Makes about 1½ cups (375ml).

■ Sauce can be made a day ahead.
■ Storage: Covered, in refrigerator.
■ Freeze: Not suitable.
■ Microwave: Not suitable.
*Also suitable for: Lamb, pork, veal,
beef.*

CHILLI GARLIC DIPPING SAUCE

⅓ cup (80ml) soy sauce
2 tablespoons dry sherry
½ small fresh red chilli,
   seeded, chopped
1 teaspoon mild sweet chilli sauce
2 cloves garlic, sliced
1 tablespoon grated fresh ginger
1 tablespoon chopped
   fresh coriander

Combine all ingredients in bowl, cover;
stand 30 minutes before serving. Served
here with chicken rissoles.

Serves 4. Makes about ¾ cup (180ml).

■ Sauce can be made a day ahead.
■ Storage: Covered, in refrigerator.
■ Freeze: Not suitable.
Also suitable for: Beef, pork, tempura.

PIQUANT SAUCE

1 tablespoon olive oil
1 small (80g) onion, finely chopped
½ teaspoon chicken stock powder
1 cup (250ml) dry white wine
1 cup (250ml) orange juice
⅓ cup (80ml) lemon juice
1½ tablespoons brown sugar
2 tablespoons orange marmalade
1 teaspoon cornflour
2 teaspoons water
¼ cup flaked almonds, toasted
1 tablespoon chopped fresh parsley

Heat oil in pan, add onion, cook, stirring,
until soft. Add stock powder, wine, juices,
sugar and marmalade, stir over heat,
without boiling, until sugar is dissolved.
Simmer, uncovered, about 10 minutes or
until reduced by half. Stir in blended
cornflour and water, stir over heat until
sauce boils and thickens slightly. Just
before serving, stir in nuts and parsley.
Served here with chicken kebabs.

Serves 4. Makes about 1¼ cups (310ml).

■ Sauce can be made a day ahead.
■ Storage: Covered, in refrigerator.
■ Freeze: Not suitable.
■ Microwave: Not suitable.
Also suitable for: Fish, veal.

*ABOVE: From back: Mushroom and Port
Sauce, Coconut and Peanut Sauce,
Lychee Sauce.*
*RIGHT: From back: Chilli Garlic Dipping
Sauce, Piquant Sauce.*

Above: Tiles from Fred Pazotti Pty Ltd.
Right: Setting from The Design Store, Mosman.

CREAMY TARRAGON AND MUSHROOM SAUCE

30g butter
250g button mushrooms, sliced
¼ cup (60ml) dry white wine
1 tablespoon brandy
300ml cream
1 teaspoon cornflour
2 teaspoons water
1 tablespoon chopped fresh chives
1 teaspoon dried tarragon

Heat butter in pan, add mushrooms, cook, stirring, until soft. Add wine and brandy, simmer, uncovered, 5 minutes, stir in cream and blended cornflour and water. Stir constantly over heat until sauce boils and thickens; stir in herbs. Served here with chicken rissoles.

Serves 4. Makes about 2 cups (500ml).

- Sauce best made close to serving.
- Freeze: Not suitable.
- Microwave: Suitable.

Also suitable for: Pasta, beef.

CURRY BUTTER

2 egg yolks
2 teaspoons curry powder
1 tablespoon lemon juice
1 clove garlic, crushed
1 teaspoon dry mustard
150g butter, melted
1 tablespoon hot water,
    approximately

Blend or process egg yolks, curry powder, juice, garlic and mustard until smooth. With motor operating, pour in hot bubbling butter a little at a time, blend until mixture is thickened. Transfer mixture to bowl, stir in enough hot water to make a thin sauce. Served here with chicken breasts.

Serves 4. Makes about ¾ cup (180ml).

- Recipe best made just before serving.
- Freeze: Not suitable.
- Microwave: Butter suitable.

Also suitable for: Seafood, vegetables.

RIGHT: From left: Creamy Tarragon and Mushroom Sauce, Curry Butter.

BACON AND SAGE SAUCE

1 tablespoon vegetable oil
2 medium (340g) red Spanish
    onions, sliced
3 cloves garlic, crushed
4 bacon rashers, thinly sliced
1 cup (250ml) water
1 small chicken stock cube
1/3 cup (80ml) dry white wine
2 teaspoons seeded mustard
1/3 cup (80ml) cream
2 tablespoons chopped fresh sage

Heat oil in pan, add onions, garlic and
bacon, cook, stirring, until onions are soft
and bacon is browned. Add water,
crumbled stock cube, wine and mustard.
Simmer, uncovered, 6 minutes. Add
cream and sage, stir over heat until thickened slightly.

Serves 6. Makes about 2 cups (500ml).
■ Recipe best made close to serving.
■ Freeze: Not suitable.
■ Microwave: Not suitable.
Also suitable for: Veal.

FIG AND PORT SAUCE

1/2 cup (125ml) water
1/2 cup (125ml) dry white wine
1 teaspoon chicken stock powder
2 dried figs, chopped
2/3 cup (160ml) cream
1/2 teaspoon cornflour
1 teaspoon water, extra
2 teaspoons port
1 tablespoon chopped fresh chives

Combine water, wine, stock powder and
figs in pan. Bring to boil, simmer, uncovered, until reduced by half. Add cream
and blended cornflour and extra water,
simmer, uncovered, until thickened slightly;
stir in port and chives.

Serves 4. Makes about 1 cup (250ml).
■ Sauce best made just before serving.
■ Freeze: Not suitable.
■ Microwave: Not suitable.
Also suitable for: Pork.

APPLE AND GINGER SAUCE

40g butter
2 tablespoons brown sugar
1 medium (150g) apple, peeled, sliced
1 tablespoon grated fresh ginger
1/4 cup (60ml) Calvados
1 cup (250ml) chicken stock
1/4 cup (60ml) clear apple juice
1/4 cup (60ml) cream
2 tablespoons chopped fresh sage
1 1/2 teaspoons cornflour
2 teaspoons water

Heat butter and sugar in pan, add apple,
cook, stirring, until lightly browned and
tender; remove apple with slotted spoon.
Add ginger and Calvados to same pan,
simmer, uncovered, until almost all liquid
is evaporated. Stir in stock, juice, cream
and sage, simmer, uncovered, 5 minutes.
Stir in blended cornflour and water, stir
over heat until sauce boils and thickens.
Return apple to sauce; stir until heated
through. Served here with duck breast fillets.

Serves 4. Makes about 1 1/2 cups (375ml).
■ Recipe best made just before serving.
■ Freeze: Not suitable.
■ Microwave: Not suitable.
Also suitable for: Pork.

MUSHROOM THYME SAUCE

1 tablespoon vegetable oil
1 clove garlic, crushed
2 green shallots, chopped
150g button mushrooms, sliced
1/2 small (75g) red pepper, chopped
1/2 teaspoon chicken stock powder
1/2 cup (125ml) dry white wine
2/3 cup (160ml) cream
2 teaspoons chopped fresh thyme
1/2 teaspoon cornflour
1 teaspoon water.

Heat oil in pan, add garlic, shallots, mushrooms and pepper, cook, stirring, until
shallots are soft. Stir in stock powder and
wine, simmer, uncovered, until reduced
by half. Stir in cream, thyme and blended
cornflour and water, stir over heat until
sauce boils and thickens slightly.

Serves 4. Makes about 2 cups (500ml)
■ Recipe can be made a day ahead.
■ Storage: Covered, in refrigerator.
■ Freeze: Not suitable.
■ Microwave: Suitable.
Also suitable for: Veal, pork.

GINGER SOY SAUCE

2 teaspoons vegetable oil
2 star anise, cracked
2 cloves garlic, crushed
8cm (50g) piece fresh ginger,
    peeled, chopped
2 green shallots, chopped
2 tablespoons soy sauce
1 cup firmly packed fresh
    coriander leaves
1 litre (4 cups) chicken stock
2 teaspoons cornflour
1 tablespoon water

Heat oil in pan, add star anise, cook, stirring, until fragrant. Add garlic, ginger and
shallots, cook, stirring, 1 minute. Add
sauce, coriander and stock, simmer, uncovered, 20 minutes. Strain sauce, return to
pan, stir in blended cornflour and water,
stir over heat until sauce boils and thickens. Served here with duck breast.

Serves 4. Makes about 2 cups (500ml).
■ Sauce can be made a day ahead.
■ Storage: Covered, in refrigerator.
■ Freeze: Not suitable.
■ Microwave: Not suitable.
Also suitable for: Beef, lamb, pork.

*LEFT: Clockwise from back: Fig and Port Sauce,
Bacon and Sage Sauce, Apple and Ginger Sauce.
RIGHT: From back: Ginger Soy Sauce,
Mushroom Thyme Sauce.*

*Left: Saucepans from Alan Tillsley Antiques,
ladle and milk warmer from The Cottage Manner.
Right: Pottery from Kenwick Galleries.*

TAMARILLO SAUCE

8 medium tamarillos, chopped
½ cup (100g) firmly packed
  brown sugar
¼ cup (60ml) water
¾ cup (180ml) beef stock
½ teaspoon five-spice powder
⅓ cup (80ml) water, extra
1 tablespoon brown sugar, extra

Combine tamarillos, sugar and water in pan, simmer, covered, about 5 minutes or until tamarillos are soft. Blend or process mixture; strain. Return mixture to pan, stir in stock, spice, extra water and extra sugar, simmer, uncovered, 5 minutes. Served here with roast duck.

Serves 4 to 6. Makes about 3½ cups (875ml).

■ Recipe can be made 2 days ahead.
■ Storage: Covered, in refrigerator.
■ Freeze: Suitable.
■ Microwave: Suitable.

Also suitable for: Ham, pork.

PROSCIUTTO AND TOMATO SAUCE

60g butter
1 medium (150g) onion, thinly sliced
1 stick celery, thinly sliced
½ medium (100g) red pepper, sliced
10 slices (about 100g) prosciutto
425g can tomatoes
⅓ cup (80ml) dry red wine
½ cup (125ml) chicken stock
2 tablespoons tomato paste
2 tablespoons chopped fresh parsley

Heat butter in pan, add onion, celery, pepper and half the prosciutto, cook, stirring, until onion is soft. Add undrained crushed tomatoes, wine, stock and paste, simmer, uncovered, until slightly thickened; stir in parsley. Just before serving, add remaining prosciutto to dry pan, cook, stirring, until browned and crisp. Serve sauce topped with prosciutto. Served here with spatchcock.

Serves 4. Makes about 2 cups (500ml).

■ Sauce can be made a day ahead.
■ Storage: Covered, in refrigerator.
■ Freeze: Not suitable.
■ Microwave: Suitable.

Also suitable for: Lamb, pasta, veal.

LEFT: From top: Tamarillo Sauce, Prosciutto and Tomato Sauce.
ABOVE RIGHT: From left: Grape Sauce, Spicy Coconut Sauce.

GRAPE SAUCE

20g butter
1 tablespoon plain flour
1 cup (250ml) dark grape juice
1 tablespoon port
¼ cup (60ml) chicken stock
2 teaspoons Worcestershire sauce
200g dark grapes
2 green shallots, sliced

Melt butter in pan, add flour, cook, stirring, until lightly browned. Remove pan from heat, stir in juice, port, stock and Worcestershire. Stir over heat until sauce boils and thickens slightly; stir in grapes and shallots. Served here with roast chicken.

Serves 4. Makes about 2 cups (500ml).

▨ Sauce can be made a day ahead.
▨ Storage: Covered, in refrigerator.
▨ Freeze: Not suitable.
▨ Microwave: Suitable.

Also suitable for: Game.

SPICY COCONUT SAUCE

2 teaspoons vegetable oil
1 small (80g) onion, finely chopped
1 clove garlic, crushed
2 teaspoons finely chopped fresh lemon grass
1 tablespoon ground coriander
2 teaspoons ground cumin
½ teaspoon ground cardamom
¼ teaspoon ground cloves
¼ teaspoon chilli powder
1 teaspoon chicken stock powder
400ml can coconut cream
2 teaspoons soy sauce
2 tablespoons chopped fresh coriander

Heat oil in pan, add onion and garlic, cook, stirring, until onion is soft. Add lemon grass, ground coriander, cumin, cardamom, cloves, chilli powder and stock powder, cook, stirring, until fragrant. Add coconut cream and soy sauce, bring to boil, simmer, uncovered, 10 minutes; stir in fresh coriander. Served here with chicken Maryland pieces.

Serves 4. Makes about 1½ cups (375ml).

▨ Recipe can be made a day ahead.
▨ Storage: Covered, in refrigerator.
▨ Freeze: Not suitable.
▨ Microwave: Suitable.

Also suitable for: Lamb, pork, vegetables.

CREAMY PEPPERCORN SAUCE

300ml cream
2 tablespoons dry white wine
2 tablespoons drained green peppercorns
1 small chicken stock cube
1 teaspoon French mustard
2 teaspoons cornflour
1 teaspoon water
1 tablespoon chopped fresh chives

Combine cream, wine, peppercorns, crumbled stock cube, mustard and blended cornflour and water in pan, stir over heat until mixture boils and thickens slightly; stir in chives. Served here with turkey breast slices.

Serves 4. Makes about 1½ cups (375ml).

■ Sauce can be made a day ahead.
■ Storage: Covered, in refrigerator.
■ Freeze: Not suitable.
■ Microwave: Suitable.
Also suitable for: Veal.

BEETROOT GLAZE

3 medium (480g) fresh beetroot
4cm piece (30g) fresh ginger, peeled, chopped
4 cloves
4 star anise
2 tablespoons brown sugar
1 clove garlic, crushed
⅓ cup (80ml) orange juice
1 cup (250ml) chicken stock
1½ tablespoons cornflour
1 tablespoon water

Boil, steam or microwave beetroot until just tender; drain. Peel beetroot, grate coarsely. Combine ginger, cloves, star anise, brown sugar, garlic, juice, stock and blended cornflour and water in pan, stir over heat until mixture boils and thickens; strain. Return sauce to pan, add beetroot; stir until heated through. Served here with roasted quail.

Serves 4. Makes about 2 cups (500ml).

■ Sauce can be made 2 days ahead.
■ Storage: Covered, in refrigerator.
■ Freeze: Not suitable.
■ Microwave: Suitable.
Also suitable for: Lamb, pork.

GINGER LEMON SAUCE

1 medium (150g) lemon
1 cup (250ml) chicken stock
2 tablespoons dry sherry
2 teaspoons soy sauce
1/3 cup (75g) sugar
1/3 cup (80ml) lemon juice
8cm piece (50g) fresh ginger, sliced
1 tablespoon cornflour
1 tablespoon water

Using a vegetable peeler, peel rind thinly from lemon. Cut rind into thin strips. Combine rind, stock, sherry, soy sauce, sugar, juice and ginger in pan. Stir over heat, without boiling, until sugar is dissolved, simmer, uncovered, 10 minutes; strain liquid, discard rind and ginger. Return liquid to pan, stir in blended cornflour and water, stir over heat until sauce boils and thickens. Served here with chicken pieces.

Serves 4. Makes about 1 cup (250ml).

■ Sauce can be made a day ahead.
■ Storage: Covered, in refrigerator.
■ Freeze: Not suitable.
■ Microwave: Suitable.

Also suitable for: Seafood, veal.

MUSTARD SAFFRON SAUCE

1 small (80g) onion, finely chopped
1/2 cup (125ml) dry white wine
small pinch saffron powder
300ml cream
1/3 cup (80ml) sour cream
1 tablespoon seeded mustard
1 teaspoon chicken stock powder
60g butter, chopped

Combine onion, wine and saffron in pan, simmer, uncovered, about 5 minutes or until reduced by half. Add creams, mustard and stock powder, simmer, uncovered, until thickened slightly. Blend or process sauce until smooth, add butter in small pieces; blend until combined. Served here with chicken breasts.

Serves 4. Makes about 1 1/2 cups (375ml).

■ Sauce best made close to serving.
■ Freeze: Not suitable.
■ Microwave: Not suitable.

Also suitable for: Veal, pork.

ABOVE: From left: Creamy Peppercorn Sauce, Beetroot Glaze.
RIGHT: From back: Mustard Saffron Sauce, Ginger Lemon Sauce.

Above: Tiles from Fred Pazotti Pty Ltd. Right: Tiles from Country Floors; china from Royal Doulton.

SHERRY CREAM SAUCE

1 bunch (about 250g) fresh asparagus
100g snow peas
1 tablespoon light olive oil
1 medium (350g) leek, thinly sliced
2 bacon rashers, finely chopped
2 cloves garlic, crushed
½ cup (125ml) dry sherry
¾ cup (180ml) chicken stock
1 cup (250ml) cream
1 tablespoon chopped fresh thyme
2 teaspoons cornflour
2 teaspoons water

Slice asparagus and snow peas into thin strips. Heat oil in pan, add leek, bacon and garlic, cook, stirring, until leek is soft. Add sherry, simmer, uncovered, until almost all liquid is evaporated. Stir in stock, cream and thyme, simmer, uncovered, 3 minutes. Add asparagus and snow peas, simmer, uncovered, until vegetables are just tender. Stir in blended cornflour and water, stir over heat until sauce boils and thickens. Served here with sliced chicken breast.

Serves 4. Makes about 3 cups (750ml).

▣ Sauce best made just before serving.
▣ Freeze: Not suitable.
▣ Microwave: Not suitable.

Also suitable for: Pasta.

ORANGE AND REDCURRANT SAUCE

2 medium (340g) oranges
½ cup (125ml) port
½ cup (125ml) redcurrant jelly
½ teaspoon French mustard
1 small chicken stock cube
2 teaspoons cornflour
1 tablespoon water

Using a vegetable peeler, peel rind thinly from half an orange. Cut rind into thin strips. Squeeze juice from both oranges (you need 1 cup/250ml juice).

Combine rind, juice, port, jelly, mustard and crumbled stock cube in pan. Simmer, uncovered, 5 minutes, stirring occasionally. Stir in blended cornflour and water, stir over heat until sauce boils and thickens

QUICK TOMATO HOLLANDAISE

2 egg yolks
1½ tablespoons white wine vinegar
250g butter, melted
1 small tomato, peeled,
**   seeded, chopped**

Combine egg yolks and vinegar in heat-proof bowl, whisk over pan of simmering water until thickened slightly. Remove from heat, gradually whisk in hot butter in thin stream while whisking continuously. (Do not whisk in white milky residue). Stir in tomato. Served here with char-grilled chicken breasts.

Serves 6. Makes about 1¼ cups (310ml).

■ Sauce must be made just
   before serving.
■ Freeze: Not suitable.
■ Microwave: Butter suitable.

Also suitable for: Beef, seafood,
vegetables.

TUNA MAYONNAISE

1 egg yolk
1 teaspoon Dijon mustard
1 clove garlic, crushed
½ cup (125ml) light olive oil
3 teaspoons lemon juice
1 tablespoon drained capers,
**   chopped**
185g can tuna, drained
1 tablespoon tomato paste
¼ cup (60ml) water, approximately
1 tablespoon chopped fresh parsley
1 small tomato, chopped

Blend or process egg, mustard and garlic until smooth. Add oil gradually in a thin stream while motor is operating; add juice, capers, tuna and paste, blend until smooth. Add enough water to give desired consistency; stir in parsley. Serve sprinkled with chopped tomato. Served here with poached chicken breasts.

Serves 4. Makes about 2 cups (500ml).

■ Recipe can be made a day ahead.
■ Storage: Covered, in refrigerator.
■ Freeze: Not suitable.
■ Microwave: Not suitable.

Also suitable for: Veal, crudites.

slightly. Served here with chicken drumsticks, wrapped in bacon.

Serves 4. Makes about 2 cups (500ml).

■ Sauce can be made a day ahead.
■ Storage: Covered, in refrigerator.
■ Freeze: Not suitable.
■ Microwave: Suitable.

Also suitable for: Lamb, pork.

ABOVE: From back: Sherry Cream Sauce,
Orange and Redcurrant Sauce.
RIGHT: From back: Tuna Mayonnaise, Quick
Tomato Hollandaise.

Above: Tiles from Fred Pazotti Pty Ltd. Right: Pan,
basket and bowl available from Home Sweet Home.

SUN-DRIED TOMATO TAPENADE

2 tablespoons drained, chopped sun-dried tomatoes
1/3 cup (55g) seedless black olives
1 clove garlic, crushed
1 teaspoon fresh thyme leaves
1 1/2 tablespoons olive oil

Blend or process tomatoes, olives, garlic and thyme until smooth. Add oil gradually in a thin stream, with motor operating; process until smooth. Served here with char-grilled chicken breasts.

Serves 4. Makes about 1/3 cup (80ml).

- Recipe can be made a week ahead.
- Storage: Covered, in refrigerator.
- Freeze: Not suitable.

Also suitable for: Game, beef, crudites.

ORANGE SAUCE

1 medium (170g) orange
1 tablespoon sugar
2 teaspoons white vinegar
2 cups (500ml) water
2 small chicken stock cubes
1/2 cup (125ml) orange juice
2 teaspoons lemon juice
3 teaspoons cornflour
1/2 cup (125ml) sweet sherry
1/4 cup (60ml) Grand Marnier

Using a vegetable peeler, peel rind thinly from orange. Cut rind into thin strips. Add rind to pan of boiling water, boil, uncovered, 3 minutes; drain. Combine rind, sugar, vinegar, water, crumbled stock cubes and juices in pan, boil, uncovered, until reduced by half. Stir in blended cornflour and sherry, stir over heat until sauce boils and thickens; stir in liqueur. Served here with roast duck breasts.

Serves 4. Makes 1 1/2 cups (375ml).

- Sauce can be made a day ahead.
- Storage: Covered, in refrigerator.
- Freeze: Not suitable.
- Microwave: Suitable.

Also suitable for: Pork.

REDCURRANT GLAZE

3/4 cup (180ml) dry red wine
1/2 cup (125ml) redcurrant jelly
3 teaspoons white vinegar
1 tablespoon cornflour
3/4 cup (180ml) water

Combine wine, jelly and vinegar in pan, stir over heat until smooth. Stir in blended cornflour and water, stir over heat until glaze boils and thickens slightly.

Serves 4. Makes about 2 cups (500ml).

- Sauce can be made a day ahead.
- Storage: Covered, in refrigerator.
- Freeze: Not suitable.
- Microwave: Suitable.

Also suitable for: Lamb, pork.

WATERCRESS SAUCE

30g butter
4 green shallots, chopped
1 clove garlic, crushed
3 cups (100g) firmly packed watercress sprigs
2 teaspoons seeded mustard
1/2 cup (125ml) vegetable stock
1/2 cup (125ml) cream
2 teaspoons lemon juice

Heat butter in pan, add shallots, garlic and watercress, cook, stirring, until watercress is wilted. Blend or process watercress mixture and remaining ingredients until smooth. Return sauce to pan, stir over heat until heated through. Served here with poached, sliced chicken breast.

Serves 4. Makes about 1 2/3 cups (410ml)

- Recipe best made just before serving.
- Freeze: Not suitable.
- Microwave: Suitable.

Also suitable for: Fish.

LEFT: From back: Orange Sauce, Sun-Dried Tomato Tapenade.
BELOW: From back: Watercress Sauce, Redcurrant Glaze.

Left: Plates from Corso de Fiori. Below: Setting from Basic Essentials.

for seafood

SAUCES

Avoid overcooking when preparing or reheating seafood, to prevent toughening. Try these sauces with other dishes, too.

SWEET AND SOUR SAUCE

1 tablespoon vegetable oil
2 cloves garlic, crushed
¼ teaspoon ground ginger
pinch chilli powder
1 tablespoon brown sugar
2 tablespoons white vinegar
2 tablespoons fish sauce
1 medium (130g) tomato, chopped
1 small (150g) yellow pepper, sliced
½ small (75g) green pepper, sliced
1 small (70g) carrot, chopped
¾ teaspoon cornflour
1 teaspoon water

Heat oil in pan, add garlic, ginger and chilli, cook, stirring, 1 minute. Add sugar, vinegar and sauce, stir over heat until sugar is dissolved. Add tomato, simmer, uncovered, 1 minute, strain. Combine strained mixture with peppers, carrot and blended cornflour and water in pan, stir over heat until mixture boils and thickens. Simmer, uncovered, about 3 minutes or until vegetables are just tender.

Serves 4. Makes about 2 cups (500ml).

■ Sauce can be made a day ahead.
■ Storage: Covered, in refrigerator.
■ Freeze: Not suitable.
■ Microwave: Suitable.
Also suitable for: Pork.

ORANGE PARSLEY SAUCE

40g butter
1 medium (150g) onion,
    finely chopped
1 tablespoon white vinegar
1 tablespoon drained chopped capers
1 teaspoon grated orange rind
⅓ cup (80ml) orange juice
80g butter, chopped, extra
2 tablespoons chopped fresh parsley

Heat butter in pan, add onion, cook, stirring, until soft. Add vinegar, capers, rind and juice, stir over heat until boiling. Remove from heat, whisk in extra butter, a few pieces at a time; stir in parsley.

Serves 4. Makes about 1 cup (250ml).

■ Recipe best made close to serving.
■ Freeze: Not suitable.
■ Microwave: Not suitable.
Also suitable for: Chicken, veal.

RIGHT: From left: Sweet and Sour Sauce, Orange Parsley Sauce.

China from Villeroy & Boch. Basket and flower pot from Home Sweet Home.

HAZELNUT BUTTER

100g butter, chopped
2 cloves garlic, crushed
⅓ cup (40g) hazelnuts,
**   toasted, chopped**
2 tablespoons chopped fresh chives

Combine butter, garlic and hazelnuts in pan, stir over heat until butter is melted; stir in chives.

Serves 4. Makes about ¾ cup (180ml).

■ Sauce best made just before serving.
■ Freeze: Not suitable.
■ Microwave: Suitable.

Also suitable for: Chicken.

RICH MORNAY SAUCE

6 cloves
1 small (80g) onion
3 cups (750ml) milk
40g butter
¼ cup (35g) plain flour
¼ cup (40g) grated gruyere cheese
½ teaspoon dry mustard
pinch cayenne pepper
2 egg yolks
¼ cup (60ml) cream

Press cloves into onion. Place onion and milk in pan, bring to boil over low heat, remove from heat, strain; discard onion.

Melt butter in pan, stir in flour, stir over heat until dry and grainy. Remove from heat, gradually stir in milk, stir over heat until mixture boils and thickens. Add cheese, mustard and pepper, stir until cheese is melted. Remove from heat, stir in egg yolks and cream.

Serves 6. Makes about 3 cups (750ml).

■ Sauce can be made a day ahead.
■ Storage: Press plastic wrap over surface; refrigerate.
■ Freeze: Not suitable.
■ Microwave: Suitable.

Also suitable for: Vegetables, chicken.

RED CHILLI AND COCONUT SAUCE

1 medium (150g) onion, chopped
1 clove garlic, crushed
2 tablespoons candlenuts, chopped
2 teaspoons chopped coriander root
1 tablespoon chopped fresh lemon grass
½ teaspoon grated lime rind
1 teaspoon galangal powder
½ teaspoon ground coriander
3 small fresh red chillies, seeded, chopped
¼ teaspoon shrimp paste
⅓ cup (80ml) vegetable oil
1 cup (250ml) coconut milk
1 cup (250ml) fish stock

Blend or process onion, garlic, nuts, coriander, lemon grass, rind, spices, chillies and paste.

Transfer mixture to small pan, stir in oil, cook slowly over low heat 1 hour, stirring occasionally. Stir in milk and stock. Simmer, uncovered, over low heat about 1 hour or until sauce is thick.

Serves 8. Makes about 2 cups (500ml).

■ Sauce can be made a day ahead.
■ Storage: Covered, in refrigerator.
■ Freeze: Not suitable.
■ Microwave: Not suitable.

MUSTARD AND WHITE WINE SAUCE

1 cup (250ml) dry white wine
1½ teaspoons drained green peppercorns
300ml cream
2 teaspoons French mustard
1½ teaspoons cornflour
2 teaspoons water

Combine wine and peppercorns in pan, simmer, uncovered, until reduced by a third. Stir in cream, mustard and blended cornflour and water; stir over heat until mixture boils and thickens.

Serves 4. Makes about 1½ cups (375ml).

■ Recipe best made close to serving.
■ Freeze: Not suitable.
■ Microwave: Suitable.

Also suitable for: Beef, pork, vegetables.

LEFT: From left: Hazelnut Butter, Rich Mornay Sauce.
RIGHT: From top: Red Chilli and Coconut Sauce, Mustard and White Wine Sauce.

Left: Serving ware from Corso de Fiori.

ONION AND OLIVE SAUCE

2 medium (400g) red peppers
2 tablespoons light olive oil
2 medium (300g) onions, sliced
2 cloves garlic, sliced
4 medium (500g) tomatoes, peeled,
   seeded, sliced
1/2 cup (80g) sliced seedless
   black olives
1 tablespoon chopped fresh thyme
2 tablespoons chopped fresh oregano
2 tablespoons balsamic vinegar
pinch sugar
2 tablespoons light olive oil, extra

Quarter peppers, remove seeds and membrane. Grill peppers, skin side up, until skin blisters and blackens. Peel away skin, slice peppers.

Heat oil in pan, add onions and garlic, cook, stirring, until onions are soft. Stir in peppers, tomatoes, olives, herbs, vinegar and sugar, cook, stirring, 5 minutes; stir in extra oil.

Serves 4. Makes about 3 1/2 cups (875ml).

■ Sauce can be made a day ahead.
■ Storage: Covered, in refrigerator.
■ Freeze: Not suitable.
■ Microwave: Not suitable.

Also suitable for: Lamb, pasta, veal, chicken.

BACON AND SPINACH SAUCE

20g butter
4 green shallots, chopped
4 bacon rashers, chopped
2 cups (500ml) cream
2 teaspoons chopped fresh thyme
3 teaspoons lemon juice
1/2 bunch (about 325g) English
   spinach, shredded
70g soft butter, chopped, extra

Heat butter in pan, add shallots and bacon, cook, stirring, until bacon is lightly browned. Add cream, thyme and juice, simmer, uncovered, until reduced by a third. Stir in spinach, cook until spinach is wilted. Remove pan from heat, gradually whisk in extra butter a small piece at a time.

Serves 6. Makes about 3 cups (750ml).

■ Recipe best made just before serving.
■ Freeze: Not suitable.
■ Microwave: Not suitable.

Also suitable for: Chicken, pasta.

HONEY CHILLI SAUCE

1/4 cup (60ml) honey
2 teaspoons mild sweet chilli sauce
2 teaspoons soy sauce
1/2 teaspoon grated fresh ginger
2/3 cup (160ml) fish stock
3 teaspoons cornflour
1/3 cup (60ml) dry white wine
1 green shallot, chopped

Combine honey, sauces, ginger, stock and blended cornflour and wine in pan, stir over heat until mixture boils and thickens; stir in shallot.

Serves 4. Makes about 1 1/3 cups (330ml).

■ Sauce can be made a day ahead.
■ Storage: Covered, in refrigerator.
■ Freeze: Not suitable.
■ Microwave: Suitable.

CHILLI BLACK BEAN SAUCE

1 tablespoon vegetable oil
1 medium (150g) onion, sliced
1 clove garlic, crushed
1 canned pimiento, drained, sliced
1/4 teaspoon sambal oelek
1 1/2 tablespoons black bean sauce
1 teaspoon sugar
1/2 cup (125ml) water
1 teaspoon cornflour
1 teaspoon water, extra
2 teaspoons chopped fresh
   coriander

Heat oil in pan, add onion and garlic, cook, stirring, until onion is soft. Add pimiento, sambal oelek, sauce, sugar, water and blended cornflour and extra water. Stir over heat until sauce boils and thickens slightly; stir in coriander.

Serves 4. Makes about 1 cup (250ml).

■ Best made just before serving.
■ Freeze: Not suitable.
■ Microwave: Suitable.

Also suitable for: Beef, chicken, pork.

LEFT: Clockwise from top left: Onion and Olive Sauce, Honey Chilli Sauce, Bacon and Spinach Sauce.
RIGHT: Chilli Black Bean Sauce.

Left: Serving ware from Accoutrement; tiles from Country Floors. Right: Plates from G. and C. Ventura.

TEMPURA DIPPING SAUCE

⅓ cup (80ml) water
⅓ cup (80ml) soy sauce
2 tablespoons mirin
½ teaspoon sugar
1 tablespoon white vinegar
1 small fresh red chilli,
    seeded, chopped

Combine all ingredients in bowl; mix well.

Serves 4. Makes about 1 cup (250ml) .

- Recipe can be made a week ahead.
- Storage: Covered, in refrigerator.
- Freeze: Not suitable.

Also suitable for: Vegetables.

BELOW: Tempura Dipping Sauce.
RIGHT: Clockwise from top: Seafood
Cocktail Sauce, Cucumber Sauce, Basil Aioli,
Tomato Pesto.

BASIL AIOLI

4 cloves garlic, crushed
2 egg yolks
1 cup firmly packed fresh basil leaves
1 cup (250ml) olive oil
2 tablespoons lemon juice
2 tablespoons milk, approximately

Blend or process garlic and egg yolks until smooth. Add basil and ⅓ cup (80ml) of the oil; blend until smooth. Gradually add remaining oil in thin stream with motor operating, blend until thick; add juice. Add enough milk to give desired consistency.

Serves 4. Makes about 1½ cups (375ml).

- Recipe can be made a day ahead.
- Storage: Press plastic wrap over surface; refrigerate.
- Freeze: Not suitable.

Also suitable for: Lamb, crudites.

SEAFOOD COCKTAIL SAUCE

⅓ cup (80ml) mayonnaise
2 tablespoons cream
1½ tablespoons tomato sauce
¼ teaspoon Worcestershire sauce
few drops Tabasco sauce

Combine all ingredients in bowl; mix well.

Serves 4. Makes about ⅔ cup (160ml).

- Sauce can be made 2 days ahead.
- Storage: Covered, in refrigerator.
- Freeze: Not suitable.

TOMATO PESTO

½ cup (80g) pine nuts, toasted
1 cup firmly packed fresh basil leaves
½ cup loosely packed fresh dill
½ cup chopped fresh chives
3 cloves garlic, crushed
2 medium (260g) tomatoes, chopped
¾ cup (60g) grated parmesan cheese
1 tablespoon tomato paste
½ cup (125ml) olive oil
¼ cup (60ml) water

Blend or process nuts, herbs, garlic, tomatoes, cheese and paste until smooth. Gradually add oil and water in thin stream while motor is operating; process mixture until combined.

Serves 4. Makes about 2 cups (500ml).

- Recipe can be made a day ahead.
- Storage: Press plastic wrap over surface; refrigerate.
- Freeze: Suitable.

Also suitable for: Pasta, chicken, pork, veal.

CUCUMBER SAUCE

½ cup lightly packed fresh parsley
1 small green cucumber, peeled, seeded, chopped
1 teaspoon coarse cooking salt
1 teaspoon white wine vinegar
1 teaspoon sugar
pinch paprika
¾ cup (180ml) cream

Add parsley to pan of boiling water for 1 minute; drain, rinse under cold water, squeeze dry. Combine cucumber, salt, vinegar and sugar in bowl, stand 1 hour.

Drain cucumber, reserve 1 teaspoon of liquid. Blend or process parsley, cucumber, reserved liquid and paprika until smooth. Combine cucumber mixture and cream in bowl; mix well.

Serves 4. Makes about 1¼ cups (310ml).

- Sauce best prepared an hour ahead.
- Storage: Covered, in refrigerator.
- Freeze: Not suitable.

Also suitable for: Lamb.

TOMATO TARRAGON CREAM

3 medium (390g) tomatoes, peeled, seeded, chopped
coarse cooking salt
¼ cup (60ml) cream
1 teaspoon French mustard
1 tablespoon chopped fresh tarragon
1 tablespoon chopped fresh parsley
2 teaspoons chopped fresh chervil
2 teaspoons brandy
1 teaspoon lemon juice
few drops Tabasco sauce

Place tomatoes in sieve, sprinkle with salt, stand 20 minutes. Rinse tomatoes gently under cold water; drain.

Combine remaining ingredients in bowl; mix well. Stir in tomatoes.

Serves 4. Makes about 1¼ cups (310ml).

▨ Recipe can be made 3 hours ahead.
▨ Storage: Covered, in refrigerator.
▨ Freeze: Not suitable.

Also suitable for: Chicken, lamb.

DILL AND MUSTARD CREAM

1 drained anchovy fillet, chopped
1 clove garlic, crushed
1 tablespoon Dijon mustard
2 tablespoons white wine vinegar
1 egg yolk
1 cup (250ml) olive oil
¼ cup (60ml) cream
2 tablespoons lemon juice
¼ cup chopped fresh dill
1 tablespoon water, approximately

Blend or process anchovy, garlic, mustard, vinegar and egg yolk until smooth. Add oil in a thin stream while motor is operating, process until thick. Add cream, process until just combined. Transfer mixture to bowl, stir in juice and dill and enough water to give desired consistency.

Serves 4. Makes about 1¾ cups (430ml).

▨ Sauce can be made a day ahead.
▨ Storage: Covered, in refrigerator.
▨ Freeze: Not suitable.

Also suitable for: Chicken.

LEFT: From left: Dill and Mustard Cream, Tomato Tarragon Cream.

Tiles from Fred Pazotti Pty Ltd.

FENNEL CREAM

20g butter
1 medium (150g) onion,
   finely chopped
1 clove garlic, crushed
½ medium (200g) fennel bulb,
   thinly sliced
1 tablespoon plain flour
¼ cup (60ml) dry white wine
1 cup (250ml) milk
1 cup (250ml) cream
1 tablespoon chopped fresh tarragon
1 teaspoon grated lemon rind

Heat butter in pan, add onion and garlic, cook, stirring, until onion is soft. Add fennel, cook, stirring, until tender. Stir in flour, stir over heat until well combined. Remove pan from heat, gradually stir in combined wine, milk, cream, tarragon and rind; stir over heat until sauce boils and thickens slightly.

Serves 4 to 6. Makes about 3 cups (750ml).

- Sauce can be made a day ahead.
- Storage: Covered, in refrigerator.
- Freeze: Not suitable.
- Microwave: Suitable.

Also suitable for: Chicken, veal.

LEMON GRASS AND SPINACH SAUCE

½ bunch (about 325g) English
   spinach, shredded
30g butter
1 small (80g) onion, finely chopped
¼ cup (60ml) dry white wine
⅓ cup (about 4 stems) chopped
   fresh lemon grass
300ml cream
90g butter, chopped, extra

Boil, steam or microwave spinach until just wilted; drain well. Heat butter in pan, add onion, cook, stirring, until soft. Add wine and lemon grass, simmer, uncovered, about 5 minutes or until reduced by half. Add cream, simmer until slightly thickened. Strain mixture into blender, add extra butter a little at a time while motor is operating. Return sauce to pan, stir in spinach, stir until heated through; do not boil.

Serves 4. Makes about 1 cup (250ml).

- Recipe best made just before serving.
- Freeze: Not suitable.
- Microwave: Spinach suitable.

Also suitable for: Chicken, veal.

LEFT: From top: Fennel Cream, Lemon Grass and Spinach Sauce.

China from Noritake.

SWEET GINGER SAUCE

⅓ cup (80ml) sweet dessert wine
½ cup (125ml) fish stock
2 teaspoons grated fresh ginger
2 teaspoons port
⅔ cup (160ml) cream
1 teaspoon cornflour
2 teaspoons water
2 green shallots, chopped

Heat half the wine in pan, boil, uncovered, until reduced by half. Add stock, ginger, port and cream, simmer, uncovered, until thickened slightly. Add remaining wine, blended cornflour and water and shallots; stir over heat until sauce boils and thickens slightly.

Serves 4. Makes about 1 cup (250ml).

■ Recipe best made just before serving.
■ Freeze: Not suitable.
■ Microwave: Not suitable.

Also suitable for: Pork, chicken.

CREAMY WATERCRESS SAUCE

2 tablespoons olive oil
1 medium (150g) onion, chopped
1 clove garlic, crushed
½ cup (125ml) dry white wine
½ cup (125ml) fish stock
300ml cream
1½ teaspoons cornflour
2 teaspoons water
1½ cups (75g) firmly packed watercress

Heat oil in pan, add onion and garlic, cook, stirring, until onion is soft. Add wine and stock, boil, uncovered, until reduced by a third. Add cream and blended cornflour and water, stir over heat until mixture boils and thickens. Remove from heat, add watercress. Blend or process mixture until smooth, return to pan, stir over heat until slightly thickened.

Serves 4. Makes about 2 cups (500ml).

■ Recipe best made close to serving.
■ Freeze: Not suitable.
■ Microwave: Not suitable.

BELOW: From left: Creamy Watercress Sauce, Sweet Ginger Sauce.

Tiles from Fred Pazotti Pty Ltd.

CHIVE BUTTER

1 tablespoon white vinegar
1 tablespoon lemon juice
3 egg yolks
1 teaspoon Dijon mustard
250g butter, chopped
1 tablespoon cream
2 tablespoons chopped fresh chives

Combine vinegar and juice in heatproof bowl, place bowl over pan of boiling water, whisk in egg yolks and mustard. Gradually whisk in butter, a few pieces at a time, whisk until butter is melted before next addition. Whisk in cream and chives.

Serves 4. Makes about 1¾ cups (430ml).

- ■ Recipe best made just before serving.
- ■ Freeze: Not suitable.
- ■ Microwave: Not suitable.

Also suitable for: Chicken, pork, veal vegetables.

MILD CURRY SAUCE

15g butter
1 small (80g) onion, chopped
1 stick celery, chopped
1 clove garlic, crushed
1½ tablespoons plain flour
1 teaspoon sugar
½ teaspoon curry powder
1½ cups (375ml) fish stock
¼ teaspoon sambal oelek
2 medium (260g) tomatoes, peeled, chopped
1 tablespoon tomato paste
½ small (75g) red pepper, chopped
½ small (75g) green pepper, chopped
1½ cups (125g) frozen green peas
1 tablespoon chopped fresh coriander

Heat butter in pan, add onion, celery and garlic, cook, stirring, until onion is soft. Stir in flour, sugar and curry powder, stir over heat until well combined. Stir in stock and sambal oelek, simmer, uncovered, 20 minutes. Add tomatoes, paste, peppers and peas, simmer, uncovered, about 2 minutes or until vegetables are tender; stir in coriander.

Serves 4 to 6. Makes about 1 litre (4 cups).

- ■ Recipe can be made a day ahead.
- ■ Storage: Covered, in refrigerator.
- ■ Freeze: Not suitable.
- ■ Microwave: Not suitable.

Also suitable for: Sausages, chicken.

OLIVE AND SUN-DRIED TOMATO SAUCE

¼ cup (60ml) olive oil
1 medium (150g) onion, finely chopped
½ teaspoon sambal oelek
2 cloves garlic, crushed
1½ drained anchovy fillets, finely chopped
⅓ cup (55g) chopped seedless green olives
¼ cup (35g) drained chopped sun-dried tomatoes
2 tablespoons drained chopped capers
1 tablespoon lemon juice
1 tablespoon olive oil, extra
2 tablespoons pine nuts, toasted
2 tablespoons shredded fresh basil leaves

Heat oil in pan, add onion, sambal oelek and garlic, cook, stirring, until onion is soft. Stir in anchovies, olives, tomatoes, capers and juice, cook, stirring, 5 minutes. Add extra oil, nuts and basil; stir until sauce is hot.

Serves 4. Makes about 1 cup (250ml).

- ■ Sauce can be made a day ahead.
- ■ Storage: Covered, in refrigerator.
- ■ Freeze: Not suitable.
- ■ Microwave: Suitable.

Also suitable for: Lamb, chicken.

LEFT: Clockwise from left: Chive Butter, Olive and Sun-Dried Tomato Sauce, Mild Curry Sauce.

China from Royal Doulton.

LEMON AND SZECHWAN PEPPER SAUCE

2 green shallots, chopped
2 tablespoons white wine vinegar
1/2 cup (125ml) dry white wine
1 teaspoon Szechwan pepper
125g butter, chopped
1 tablespoon cream

Combine shallots, vinegar, wine and pepper in small pan. Simmer, uncovered, until mixture is reduced to 1/4 cup (60ml). Whisk in butter quickly, a few pieces at a time, over low heat until all butter is incorporated. Add cream; mix well. Strain mixture through coarse sieve.

Serves 4. Makes about 3/4 cup (180ml).

◼ Recipe best made just before serving.
◼ Freeze: Not suitable.
◼ Microwave: Not suitable.

Also suitable for: Chicken.

ANCHOVY CAPER MAYONNAISE

4 canned drained anchovy
fillets, chopped
2 green shallots, chopped
2 tablespoons chopped fresh parsley
2 tablespoons drained capers
1 clove garlic, crushed
1 teaspoon sugar
1 tablespoon lemon juice
2/3 cup (160ml) olive oil
2 egg yolks

Blend anchovies, shallots, parsley, capers, garlic, sugar, juice and 2 table-spoons of the oil until combined. Add egg yolks, blend until well combined. Gradually add remaining oil in a thin stream while motor is operating.

Serves 4. Makes about 1 1/4 cups (310ml).

◼ Recipe can be made a day ahead.
◼ Storage: Covered, in refrigerator.
◼ Freeze: Not suitable.
Also suitable for: Vegetables, beef.

ABOVE: From left: Anchovy Caper Mayonnaise, Lemon and Szechwan Pepper Sauce.
RIGHT: From top: Tandoori Sauce, Prawn and Port Sauce.

TANDOORI SAUCE

1 teaspoon paprika
1 teaspoon ground cinnamon
1 teaspoon turmeric
1 teaspoon seasoned pepper
1 teaspoon ground coriander
2 teaspoons fennel seeds
2 tablespoons grated fresh ginger
2 teaspoons sambal oelek
1⅓ cups (330ml) plain yogurt

Combine paprika, cinnamon, turmeric, pepper, coriander and seeds in dry pan, stir over heat until fragrant; cool. Combine spices, ginger, sambal oelek and yogurt; mix well. Reserve 1 cup (250ml) of yogurt mixture. Brush remaining mixture over your choice of fish, cover, refrigerate 2 hours. Place fish on wire rack in baking dish, bake, uncovered, in moderate oven until tender. Serve with reserved sauce.

Serves 4.

■ Sauce can be made 2 days ahead.
■ Storage: Covered, in refrigerator.
■ Freeze: Not suitable.
■ Microwave: Not suitable.

Also suitable for: Chicken, lamb, pork.

PRAWN AND PORT SAUCE

500g uncooked prawns
1 tablespoon light olive oil
1 clove garlic, chopped
1 medium (125g) carrot, chopped
1 stick celery, chopped
1 medium (150g) onion, chopped
¼ cup (60ml) port
2 tablespoons brandy
1 cup (250ml) dry white wine
1 cup (250ml) water
3 medium (390g) tomatoes, chopped
1 tablespoon tomato paste
¼ cup (60ml) cream

Remove shells from prawns; reserve prawns for another use. Heat oil in pan, add garlic, carrot, celery and onion, cook, stirring, until onion is soft. Add prawn shells, cook, stirring, 2 minutes. Add port and brandy, simmer, uncovered, until reduced by half. Add wine, water, tomatoes and tomato paste, simmer, covered, 15 minutes.

Strain mixture through sieve, extracting as much juice as possible. Return sauce to pan, simmer, uncovered, about 20 minutes or until reduced to 1 cup (250ml). Add cream, stir until heated through.

Serves 6. Makes about 1½ cups (375ml).

■ Sauce can be made a day ahead.
■ Storage: Covered, in refrigerator.
■ Freeze: Not suitable.
■ Microwave: Not suitable.

SAUCES *for beef*

Versatile beef shines in combination with the pungent flavours of horseradish, garlic and chilli – plus a few surprises.

TARRAGON WINE SAUCE

1 tablespoon vegetable oil
4 fillet steaks
1/3 cup (80ml) dry white wine
30g butter
4 green shallots, chopped
1 teaspoon plain flour
1 teaspoon dried tarragon leaves
1/2 cup (125ml) beef stock
1/4 cup (60ml) cream

Heat oil in pan, add steaks, cook over high heat until browned and cooked as desired. Transfer steaks to dish; keep warm. Reserve pan and juices. Add wine to reserved pan juices, simmer, uncovered, until reduced by a third; remove from pan. Melt butter in same pan, add shallots, flour and tarragon, stir over heat until well combined, remove from heat, gradually stir in reserved pan juices, stock and cream, stir over heat until sauce boils and thickens.

Serves 4. Makes about 2/3 cup (160ml).

- Sauce can be made a day ahead.
- Storage: Covered, in refrigerator.
- Freeze: Not suitable.
- Microwave: Not suitable.

SPICY TOMATO SAUCE

2 tablespoons olive oil
2 large (400g) onions, chopped
2 cloves garlic, crushed
6 large (1.5kg) tomatoes, chopped
1/4 cup (60ml) dry red wine
1 teaspoon chilli powder
2 tablespoons brown sugar
1 tablespoon Dijon mustard
few drops Tabasco sauce

Heat oil in pan, add onions and garlic, cook, stirring, until onions are soft. Add tomatoes, wine, chilli and sugar, simmer, uncovered, about 30 minutes or until mixture is reduced by a third. Blend or process mixture until smooth; strain, discard skin and seeds. Return sauce to pan, stir in mustard and Tabasco; stir over heat until heated through. Served here with meatballs.

Serves 4. Makes about 2 cups (500ml).

- Sauce can be made a day ahead.
- Storage: Covered, in refrigerator.
- Freeze: Suitable.
- Microwave: Not suitable.

Also suitable for: Seafood, chicken.

LEFT: From left: Tarragon Wine Sauce, Spicy Tomato Sauce.

China from Villeroy and Boch.

GRAVY

1kg piece sirloin
1 tablespoon olive oil
2 tablespoons plain flour
¾ cup (180ml) dry red wine
1¼ cups (310ml) beef stock
1 teaspoon Worcestershire sauce

Tie beef with string at 2cm intervals. Heat oil in baking dish, add beef, cook over high heat until brown all over. Bake in moderate oven about 45 minutes or until cooked as desired. Remove beef from dish, stand 5 minutes; reserve 2 tablespoons of beef juices. Heat reserved juices in dish, add flour, stir over heat until bubbling. Remove dish from heat, gradually stir in wine, stock and Worcestershire sauce, stir over heat until mixture boils and thickens; strain.

Serves 4. Makes about 2 cups (500ml).

- Recipe best made just before serving.
- Freeze: Not suitable.
- Microwave: Not suitable.

HORSERADISH CREAM

¼ cup (60ml) horseradish relish
½ cup (125ml) cream
¼ teaspoon sugar
½ teaspoon dry mustard
2 teaspoons lemon juice

Combine all ingredients in bowl; mix well.

Serves 4. Makes about ¾ cup (180ml).

- Cream can be made a day ahead.
- Storage: Covered, in refrigerator.
- Freeze: Not suitable.

CUMQUAT RELISH SAUCE

500g cumquats, seeded, chopped
2½ cups (625ml) water
1 tablespoon black peppercorns
2 bay leaves
1 medium (150g) onion, chopped
2 tablespoons cranberry sauce
¼ cup (60ml) cider vinegar
2 teaspoons chicken stock powder
2 cloves garlic, crushed
⅓ cup (75g) sugar
1 tablespoon brandy

Combine cumquats, water, peppercorns, bay leaves, onion, cranberry sauce, vinegar, stock, garlic and sugar in large pan. Boil, uncovered, 8 minutes, simmer, uncovered, further 10 minutes or until mixture is thickened; discard bay leaves. Blend or process cumquat mixture until almost smooth; strain, stir in brandy.

Serves 8. Makes about 1½ cups (375ml).

- Recipe can be made 2 weeks ahead.
- Storage: Covered, in refrigerator.
- Freeze: Not suitable.
- Microwave: Not suitable.

Also suitable for: Lamb, pork, poultry, veal.

GREEN PEPPERCORN SAUCE

90g butter
2 tablespoons lemon juice
¼ cup (45g) drained green peppercorns
3 egg yolks
½ cup (125ml) cream
¼ cup (60ml) sour cream
1 tablespoon French mustard

Place butter, juice and peppercorns in pan, stir over heat until butter is melted; remove from heat. Whisk in remaining ingredients, whisk over low heat, without boiling, until sauce thickens slightly.

Serves 4. Makes about 1½ cups (375ml).

- Recipe best made close to serving.
- Freeze: Not suitable.
- Microwave: Not suitable.

Also suitable for: Chicken, pork.

ABOVE: Horseradish Cream accompanies roast beef served with Gravy.
RIGHT: From left: Cumquat Relish Sauce, Green Peppercorn Sauce.

Above: China from Royal Doulton. Right: Tiles from Country Floors, china from Villeroy & Boch.

CREAMY ONION SAUCE

30g butter
1 small (80g) onion, finely chopped
3 teaspoons plain flour
1 cup (250ml) milk
1 tablespoon chopped fresh parsley

Heat butter in pan, add onion, cook, stirring, until soft. Add flour, cook, stirring, until bubbling. Remove from heat, gradually stir in milk, stir over heat until sauce boils and thickens; stir in parsley. Served here with corned silverside.

Serves 4. Makes about 1 cup (250ml).

- Recipe best made close to serving.
- Freeze: Not suitable.
- Microwave: Suitable.

SATAY SAUCE

1 cup (150g) roasted unsalted
    peanuts
1 medium (150g) onion, chopped
3 cloves garlic, chopped
5cm (35g) piece fresh
    ginger, chopped
1 tablespoon chopped fresh
    lemon grass
1 small fresh red chilli, chopped
1 tablespoon grated lime rind
¼ cup chopped fresh coriander
    roots and stalks
2 teaspoons sesame oil
2 teaspoons vegetable oil
1 teaspoon cumin seeds
½ teaspoon turmeric
2 x 283ml cans coconut milk
1½ tablespoons fish sauce
3 teaspoons tamarind sauce
1½ tablespoons brown sugar

Process peanuts until finely minced. Process onion, garlic, ginger, lemon grass, chilli, rind and coriander until finely minced. Heat oils in pan, add onion mixture, cook, stirring, over low heat about 10 minutes or until fragrant. Add cumin and turmeric, cook, stirring, 1 minute. Stir in peanuts, coconut milk, sauces and sugar, simmer, uncovered, 5 minutes. Served here with meatballs.

Serves 6. Makes about 3½ cups (875ml).

- Sauce can be made a day ahead.
- Storage: Covered, in refrigerator.
- Freeze: Not suitable.
- Microwave: Suitable.

Also suitable for: Lamb, chicken, pork.

MUSTARD WINE SAUCE

30g butter
1 medium (150g) onion, sliced
3 teaspoons seeded mustard
1½ cups (310ml) beef stock
¼ cup (60ml) dry red wine
1½ tablespoons brown vinegar
60g butter, chopped, extra
2 teaspoons cornflour
2 teaspoons water

Heat butter in pan, add onion, cook, stirring, until soft. Add mustard, stock, wine, vinegar and extra butter; stir until melted. Stir in blended cornflour and water, stir over heat until mixture boils and thickens.

Serves 4. Makes about 2 cups (500ml).

- Sauce can be made 2 days ahead.
- Storage: Covered, in refrigerator.
- Freeze: Not suitable.
- Microwave: Not suitable.

Also suitable for: Lamb, pork.

TOMATO APPLE SALSA

1 tablespoon vegetable oil
1 medium (150g) apple, chopped
2 medium (260g) tomatoes, peeled,
    seeded, chopped
¼ cup (60ml) brown vinegar
¼ cup (60ml) water
1 teaspoon sugar
1 tablespoon chopped fresh
    coriander

Heat oil in pan, add apple, cook, stirring, until just tender. Add tomatoes, vinegar, water and sugar, cook, stirring, about 5 minutes or until tomatoes are just soft; stir in coriander.

Serves 4. Makes about 2 cups (500ml).

- Sauce can be made a day ahead.
- Storage: Covered, in refrigerator.
- Freeze: Not suitable.
- Microwave: Suitable.

Also suitable for: Lamb, pork, chicken.

LEFT: From back: Mustard Wine Sauce, Tomato Apple Salsa.
ABOVE: From top: Creamy Onion Sauce, Satay Sauce.

Left: Plates from Villeroy & Boch, tiles from Fred Pazotti Pty Ltd.

CREAMY CORIANDER SAUCE

½ cup (125ml) cream
½ cup (125ml) sour cream
1 clove garlic, crushed
½ teaspoon cornflour
1 teaspoon water
1 tablespoon chopped
    fresh coriander
2 teaspoons lime juice

Heat cream, sour cream and garlic in pan, stir in blended cornflour and water, stir over heat until sauce boils and thickens. Stir in coriander and juice.

Serves 4. Makes about 1 cup (250ml).

- Recipe can be made a day ahead.
- Storage: Covered, in refrigerator.
- Freeze: Not suitable.
- Microwave: Suitable.

Also suitable for: Chicken, seafood, veal.

TOMATO MUSHROOM SAUCE

1 tablespoon vegetable oil
1 medium (150g) onion, chopped
1 clove garlic, crushed
1 medium (200g) red pepper, chopped
1 teaspoon dried marjoram leaves
¼ teaspoon chilli powder
1 tablespoon brown sugar
¼ cup (60ml) dry red wine
410g can tomatoes
125g button mushrooms, sliced

Heat oil in pan, add onion and garlic, cook, stirring, until onion is soft. Stir in pepper, marjoram, chilli, sugar, wine and undrained crushed tomatoes, simmer, uncovered, until sauce is thick. Add mushrooms, simmer, uncovered, further 5 minutes. Served here with kebabs.

Serves 4. Makes about 1½ cups (375ml).

- Recipe can be made a day ahead.
- Storage: Covered, in refrigerator.
- Freeze: Suitable.
- Microwave: Suitable.

Also suitable for: Chicken, lamb, pork, veal.

RIGHT: From Left: Tomato Mushroom Sauce, Creamy Coriander Sauce.

Plates from Villeroy & Boch, tiles from Fred Pazotti Pty Ltd.

PAWPAW MAYONNAISE

2 egg yolks
1 teaspoon Dijon mustard
2 teaspoons grated lime rind
1 tablespoon lime juice
⅔ cup (160ml) vegetable oil
⅓ cup (80ml) pawpaw puree
½ teaspoon honey
1 tablespoon chopped fresh mint

Blend or process yolks, mustard, rind and juice until smooth. Gradually add oil in thin stream while motor is operating. Add pawpaw puree and honey, blend until smooth. Transfer mixture to bowl, stir in mint.

Serves 4 to 6. Makes about 1¼ cups (310ml).

▓ Recipe can be made a day ahead.
▓ Storage: Covered, in refrigerator.
▓ Freeze: Not suitable.
Also suitable for: Lamb, chicken, fish.

FRUITY RELISH

¼ cup (15g) shredded coconut
1 medium (170g) banana, chopped
½ x 425g can peach halves in syrup, drained, chopped
2 tablespoons lime juice
1 tablespoon chopped fresh mint

Combine all ingredients in bowl; mix well.

Serves 6. Makes about 1½ cups (375ml).

▓ Recipe can be made a day ahead.
▓ Storage: Covered, in refrigerator.
▓ Freeze: Not suitable.
Also suitable for: Lamb, chicken, pork.

EGGPLANT PUREE

1 small (250g) eggplant
coarse cooking salt
¼ cup (60ml) olive oil
2 cloves garlic, crushed
2 tablespoons lemon juice
2 tablespoons plain yogurt
1 tablespoon chopped fresh mint

Peel and chop eggplant, sprinkle with salt; stand 30 minutes. Rinse eggplant under cold water, drain on absorbent paper. Heat oil in pan, add eggplant and garlic, cook, stirring, about 2 minutes or until eggplant is soft. Blend or process eggplant mixture until smooth; stir in juice, yogurt and mint. Served here with meatballs.

Serves 4. Makes about 1 cup (250ml).

▓ Puree can be made 2 days ahead.
▓ Storage: Covered, in refrigerator.
▓ Freeze: Not suitable.
▓ Microwave: Not suitable.
Also suitable for: Lamb, chicken, vegetables.

THAI-STYLE SAUCE

2 tablespoons vegetable oil
1 medium (150g) onion, finely chopped
2 teaspoons curry powder
2 teaspoons finely chopped fresh ginger
1 clove garlic, crushed
1 stem fresh lemon grass, finely chopped
1 tablespoon soy sauce
400ml can coconut cream

Heat oil in pan, add onion, curry powder, ginger, garlic and lemon grass, cook, stirring, until onion is soft. Stir in soy sauce and coconut cream, simmer, uncovered, about 2 minutes or until sauce is slightly thickened. Served here with beef strips.

Serves 4 to 6. Makes about 1½ cups (375ml).

▓ Recipe can be made a day ahead.
▓ Storage: Covered, in refrigerator.
▓ Freeze: Not suitable.
▓ Microwave: Suitable.
Also suitable for: Pork, veal, chicken.

LEFT: From back: Pawpaw Mayonnaise, Fruity Relish.
BELOW: From Left: Eggplant Puree (also in jug), Thai-Style Sauce.

Left: China from Villeroy & Boch. Below: Plates from Villeroy & Boch, sauce boat from Royal Doulton.

RICH MUSHROOM SAUCE

1.4kg sirloin roast
1 tablespoon vegetable oil
1/3 cup (80ml) dry red wine
1 1/2 tablespoons plain flour
2 cups (500ml) beef stock
2 cloves garlic, crushed
350g button mushrooms, sliced
20g butter

Tie beef with string at 3cm intervals. Heat oil in large baking dish, add beef, cook, turning until browned all over. Place meat on wire rack over same baking dish. Bake, uncovered, in moderate oven about 1 hour or until cooked as desired.

Remove beef from baking dish, stand covered, 10 minutes. Drain fat from baking dish, add wine; bring to boil. Add flour, cook, stirring, 2 minutes, gradually add stock, garlic and mushrooms. Simmer, uncovered, about 3 minutes or until mushrooms are tender and sauce is thickened; whisk in butter.

Serves 6. Makes about 3 cups (750ml).

■ Recipe best made just before serving.
■ Freeze: Not suitable.
■ Microwave: Not suitable.

RED WINE SAUCE

6 French shallots, finely chopped
1/2 cup (125ml) dry red wine
2 sprigs fresh thyme
2 tablespoons tomato paste
2 cups (500ml) beef stock
2 teaspoons cornflour
1 tablespoon water
40g butter, chopped

Combine shallots, wine and thyme in small pan, simmer, uncovered, until mixture is reduced by half. Add paste and stock, simmer, uncovered, about 5 minutes or until mixture is reduced to 1 1/2 cups (375ml). Stir in blended cornflour and water, stir over heat until sauce boils and thickens. Remove from heat, whisk in butter a little at a time, until melted. Strain sauce.

Serves 4. Makes about 1 1/2 cups (375ml).

■ Sauce can be made a day ahead.
■ Storage: Covered, in refrigerator.
■ Freeze: Not suitable.
■ Microwave: Not suitable.

GINGER PLUM SAUCE

6 dried Chinese mushrooms
1 tablespoon vegetable oil
1 medium (150g) onion, thinly sliced
1 clove garlic, crushed
2 teaspoons chopped fresh ginger
1/3 cup (80ml) plum sauce
1 1/3 cups (330ml) chicken stock
3 teaspoons cornflour
1 tablespoon water
1 tablespoon chopped
    fresh coriander

Place mushrooms in bowl, cover with boiling water; stand 30 minutes. Drain mushrooms, discard stalks and slice caps. Heat oil in pan, add onion, garlic and ginger, cook, stirring, until onion is soft. Add mushrooms, sauce, stock and blended cornflour and water, cook, stirring, until mixture boils and thickens; stir in coriander.

Serves 4. Makes about 2 cups (500ml).

■ Sauce can be made a day ahead.
■ Storage: Covered, in refrigerator.
■ Freeze: Not suitable.
■ Microwave: Suitable.

Also suitable for: Lamb, chicken, veal, pork.

CHINESE VEGETABLE SAUCE

1 tablespoon vegetable oil
½ small (75g) red pepper, sliced
1 medium (125g) carrot, sliced
½ x 225g can bamboo shoots, sliced
150g button mushrooms, quartered
4 green shallots, sliced
¼ cup (60ml) soy sauce
⅓ cup (80ml) orange juice
1 clove garlic, crushed
1 teaspoon cornflour
1 small fresh red chilli, finely chopped

Heat oil in pan or wok, add pepper and carrot, stir-fry 1 minute, add bamboo shoots, mushrooms and shallots, stir-fry 2 minutes. Add combined remaining ingredients, stir-fry until mixture boils and thickens slightly.

Serves 4. Makes about 3 cups (750ml).

▓ Recipe best made just before serving.
▓ Freeze: Not suitable.
▓ Microwave: Not suitable.
Also suitable for: Chicken, pork, lamb.

ONION AND PEPPER RELISH

1 tablespoon light olive oil
1 teaspoon sesame oil
2 medium (340g) red Spanish onions, sliced
2 medium (400g) red peppers, sliced
¼ cup (60ml) red wine vinegar
½ cup (80ml) rice wine vinegar
¼ cup (60ml) mirin
¼ teaspoon dried crushed chillies
½ teaspoon cracked black pepper
2 star anise
⅓ cup (75g) sugar

Heat oils in pan, add onions and peppers, cook, covered, stirring occasionally, about 15 minutes or until onions are soft. Add remaining ingredients, simmer, uncovered, about 20 minutes or until thick.

Serves 6. Makes about 2 cups (500ml).

▓ Relish can be made 3 days ahead.
▓ Storage: Covered, in refrigerator.
▓ Freeze: Not suitable.
▓ Microwave: Not suitable.
Also suitable for: Pork, lamb, chicken.

LEFT: From left: Rich Mushroom Sauce, Red Wine Sauce.
BELOW: Clockwise from left: Onion and Pepper Relish, Chinese Vegetable Sauce, Ginger Plum Sauce.

Left: China from Royal Doulton, tiles from Country Floors.

BRANDY BLUE CHEESE SAUCE

40g butter
1 medium (150g) onion, chopped
2 tablespoons plain flour
1 cup (250ml) chicken stock
½ cup (125ml) milk
1 tablespoon brandy
200g blue cheese, crumbled
1 clove garlic, crushed

Heat butter in pan, add onion, cook, stirring, until soft. Add flour, cook, stirring, until bubbling. Remove pan from heat, gradually stir in stock, milk and brandy, stir over heat until mixture boils and thickens slightly. Blend or process the sauce with cheese and garlic until smooth.

Serves 4. Makes about 2 cups (500ml).

- Recipe can be made a day ahead.
- Storage: Covered, in refrigerator.
- Freeze: Not suitable.
- Microwave: Suitable.

Also suitable for: Vegetables, pasta.

ROASTED RED PEPPER SAUCE

3 medium (600g) red peppers
1 tablespoon olive oil
2 cloves garlic, crushed
6 small French shallots, chopped
1 cup (250ml) dry white wine
1 cup (250ml) chicken stock
1 tablespoon tomato paste

Halve peppers, remove seeds and membrane. Place peppers, skin side up on greased oven tray, bake in moderately hot oven about 30 minutes or until tender.

Cover peppers with foil; cool. Peel away skin and chop peppers. Heat oil in pan, add garlic and shallots, cook, stirring until shallots are soft. Add peppers and remaining ingredients, simmer, uncovered, 20 minutes. Blend or process mixture until smooth.

Serves 4. Makes about 2½ cups (625ml).

- Sauce can be made a day ahead.
- Storage: Covered, in refrigerator.
- Freeze: Not suitable.
- Microwave: Not suitable.

Also suitable for: Seafood, veal, lamb, vegetables.

LEFT: From top: Brandy Blue Cheese Sauce, Sweet and Sour Apricot Sauce, Roasted Red Pepper Sauce.
ABOVE RIGHT: From left: Madeira Sauce, Sour Cream with Gherkin Sauce.

Above right: Plates from Royal Doulton.

SWEET AND SOUR APRICOT SAUCE

2 tablespoons chopped dried apricots
¾ cup (180ml) water
1 green shallot, chopped
¼ cup (60ml) white vinegar
1 tablespoon honey
1½ tablespoons vegetable oil
2 tablespoons tomato sauce
¼ teaspoon soy sauce
2 tablespoons water, extra

Combine apricots and water in pan, simmer, uncovered, about 5 minutes or until soft. Blend or process undrained apricot mixture until smooth. Combine apricot puree, shallot, vinegar, honey, oil, sauces and extra water in pan, simmer, uncovered about 5 minutes or until thickened slightly.

Serves 4. Makes about 1 cup (250ml).

■ Sauce can be made a day ahead.
■ Storage: Covered, in refrigerator.
■ Freeze: Not suitable.
■ Microwave: Suitable.
Also suitable for: Chicken, pork.

MADEIRA SAUCE

50g butter
1 medium (150g) onion, chopped
1 clove garlic, crushed
2 tablespoons plain flour
3 cups (750ml) beef stock
¼ cup (60ml) Madeira
100g button mushrooms, sliced

Heat butter in pan, add onion and garlic, cook, stirring, until onion is browned. Add flour, stir over heat until flour is browned. Remove pan from heat, gradually stir in stock, stir over heat until sauce boils and thickens. Add Madeira, simmer, uncovered, 30 minutes, stirring occasionally. Push sauce through sieve. Return sauce to pan, add mushrooms, simmer, uncovered, 2 minutes.

Serves 4. Makes about 2½ cups (625ml).

■ Recipe can be made a day ahead.
■ Storage: Covered, in refrigerator.
■ Freeze: Suitable.
■ Microwave: Suitable.
Also suitable for: Veal, lamb.

SOUR CREAM WITH GHERKIN SAUCE

300ml sour cream
½ cup (100g) drained chopped gherkins
2 green shallots, finely chopped
1 tablespoon chopped fresh parsley
2 teaspoons chopped fresh tarragon
1 teaspoon cracked black pepper
½ teaspoon paprika
⅓ cup (80ml) water
¾ teaspoon sugar

Combine all ingredients in pan, stir over heat until just warm. Serve warm or cold.

Serves 4. Makes about 2 cups (500ml).

■ Sauce can be made 3 days ahead.
■ Storage: Covered, in refrigerator.
■ Freeze: Not suitable.
■ Microwave: Not suitable.
Also suitable for: Chicken, veal, seafood.

SAUCES
for lamb

Lamb needs little fat to maintain flavour and juiciness. These sauces team perfectly with cuts which have been trimmed of excess fat.

CREAMY SPINACH SAUCE

30g butter
1 small (80g) onion, sliced
½ teaspoon ground cumin
¼ bunch (about 170g) English spinach, shredded
1 tablespoon chopped fresh basil
1 tablespoon chopped fresh thyme
1 teaspoon chicken stock powder
300ml cream
1 teaspoon cornflour
2 tablespoons water

Heat butter in pan, add onion and cumin, cook, stirring, until onion is soft. Add spinach, herbs, stock powder and cream, bring to boil. Stir in blended cornflour and water, stir constantly over heat until mixture boils and thickens.

Serves 4. Makes about 1¼ cups (310ml).

■ Recipe can be made a day ahead.
■ Storage: Covered, in refrigerator.
■ Freeze: Not suitable.
■ Microwave: Suitable.

Also suitable for: Chicken, fish, pasta.

TOMATO, EGGPLANT AND OLIVE SAUCE

3 baby (180g) eggplants, sliced
vegetable oil for shallow-frying
2 tablespoons olive oil
1 large (200g) onion, sliced
3 cloves garlic, sliced
410g can tomatoes
¼ cup (60ml) dry red wine
2 tablespoons chopped fresh thyme
⅓ cup (60g) baby black olives
2 tablespoons tomato paste
½ teaspoon sugar
2 tablespoons chopped fresh parsley

Shallow-fry eggplants in hot vegetable oil until lightly browned; drain on absorbent paper. Heat olive oil in pan, add onion and garlic, cook, stirring, until onion is soft. Stir in undrained crushed tomatoes, wine, thyme, olives, paste and sugar, simmer, uncovered, about 10 minutes or until thickened slightly. Stir in eggplant and parsley; stir until heated through.

Serves 4 to 6. Makes about 3 cups (750ml).

■ Sauce can be made a day ahead.
■ Storage: Covered, in refrigerator.
■ Freeze: Not suitable.
■ Microwave: Not suitable.

Also suitable for: Chicken, beef, veal, seafood, pasta.

YOGURT AND CUCUMBER SAUCE

¾ cup (180ml) plain yogurt
1 small (120g) green cucumber, seeded, grated
1 clove garlic, crushed
1 tablespoon chopped fresh mint
2 teaspoons lemon juice

Combine all ingredients in bowl; mix well.

Serves 4. Makes about 1 cup (250ml).

■ Sauce can be made a day ahead.
■ Storage: Covered, in refrigerator.
■ Freeze: Not suitable.

Also suitable for: Chicken, vegetables, pork, fish.

RIGHT: From left: Tomato, Eggplant and Olive Sauce, Creamy Spinach Sauce, Yogurt and Cucumber Sauce.

MINT SAUCE

⅓ cup (75g) sugar
½ cup (125ml) water
1 cup (250ml) cider vinegar
¾ cup chopped fresh mint

Combine sugar and water in small pan, stir over heat, without boiling, until sugar is dissolved, boil, uncovered, about 4 minutes or until slightly thickened. Remove pan from heat, stir in vinegar and mint; stand 15 minutes. Stir well before serving.

Serves 6. Makes about 1½ cups (375ml).

- Recipe can be made a week ahead.
- Storage: Covered, in refrigerator.
- Freeze: Not suitable.
- Microwave: Not suitable.

MINT JELLY

1kg apples
1.5 litres (6 cups) water
⅓ cup (80ml) lemon juice
⅔ cup chopped fresh mint
3 cups (660g) sugar, approximately
¼ cup chopped fresh mint, extra

Chop unpeeled apples, do not discard seeds. Combine apples, seeds, water, juice and mint in large pan, simmer, covered, about 40 minutes or until apples are very soft. Strain mixture through a fine cloth into large bowl. Allow liquid to drip through cloth slowly; do not squeeze or press pulp as this will make a cloudy jelly; discard pulp. Measure apple liquid into large pan, allow ¾ cup (165g) sugar to each 1 cup (250ml) liquid (mixture should not be more than 5cm deep at this stage). Stir over heat, without boiling, until sugar is dissolved, boil, uncovered, without stirring, about 20 minutes or until jelly sets when tested on a cold saucer. Remove from heat, stand 10 minutes; skim surface. Stir in extra mint. Pour into hot sterilised jars; seal while hot.

Makes about 1 litre (4 cups).

- Storage: In cool dry cupboard for up to a year. Once open, store in refrigerator.
- Freeze: Not suitable.
- Microwave: Not suitable.

ORANGE AND PORT SAUCE

2kg leg of lamb
2 cloves garlic, sliced
3 sprigs rosemary
1 medium (170g) orange
60g butter
3 green shallots, chopped
1 cup (250ml) port
2 teaspoons honey
80g butter, extra
2 tablespoons chopped fresh mint

Using the point of a knife, make 12 incisions evenly over top of lamb. Place a slice of garlic and some rosemary leaves in each incision. Place lamb on wire rack over baking dish, bake, in moderate oven about 1¼ hours or until cooked as desired. Remove lamb from baking dish, cover, keep warm. Drain fat from baking dish; reserve dish. Using a vegetable peeler peel rind thinly from orange. Cut rind into very thin strips. Add strips to pan of boiling water, boil 3 minutes; drain. Add butter, shallots and port to reserved baking dish, simmer, uncovered, until reduced by a third, add rind and honey. Just before serving whisk in extra butter; stir in mint. Serve sauce with lamb.

Serves 6. Makes about 1 cup (250ml).

- Sauce best made just before serving.
- Freeze: Not suitable.
- Microwave: Not suitable.

SWEET PEPPER SAUCE

1 tablespoon vegetable oil
1 medium (150g) onion, chopped
1 medium (200g) red pepper, chopped
1 medium (200g) green pepper, chopped
1 stick celery, chopped
410g can tomatoes
1 teaspoon paprika
¼ cup (60ml) tomato paste
1 teaspoon beef stock powder
1 cup (250ml) water
½ teaspoon sugar

Heat oil in pan, add onion, peppers and celery, cook, stirring, until vegetables are soft. Stir in undrained crushed tomatoes and remaining ingredients,

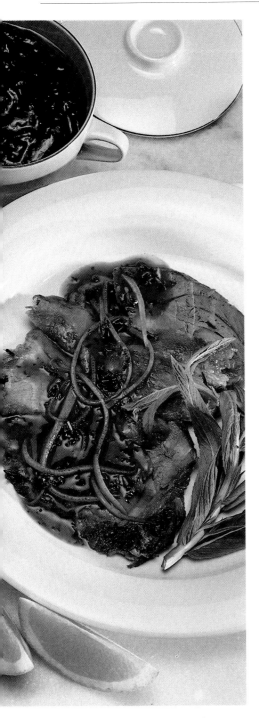

MINTED BEARNAISE SAUCE

2 tablespoons chopped fresh mint
2 tablespoons chopped
    fresh tarragon
½ cup (125ml) white vinegar
¼ cup (60ml) dry white wine
½ teaspoon black peppercorns
3 green shallots, chopped
3 egg yolks
250g butter, melted
1 tablespoon chopped fresh
    mint, extra

Combine mint, tarragon, vinegar, wine, peppercorns and shallots in pan, simmer, uncovered, about 5 minutes or until reduced to 2 tablespoons; drain. Whisk egg yolks and vinegar mixture in bowl over pan of simmering water until thick, remove from heat. Gradually whisk in hot butter in thin steady stream while whisking constantly (do not pour in white sediment from butter). Stir in extra mint.

Serves 4 to 6. Makes about 2 cups (500ml).

■ Recipe best made close to serving.
■ Freeze: Not suitable.
■ Microwave: Not suitable.

Also suitable for: Pork, veal, chicken, beef.

REMOULADE SAUCE

1 egg
1 egg yolk
1 cup (250ml) vegetable oil
2 teaspoons lemon juice
2 teaspoons Dijon mustard
1 teaspoon seeded mustard
1 tablespoon finely chopped gherkins
2 teaspoons chopped fresh tarragon
2 drained anchovy fillets,
    finely chopped

Blend or process egg and egg yolk until smooth. Add oil gradually in a thin stream while motor is operating, blend until thick and creamy. Transfer mixture to bowl, stir in remaining ingredients.

Serves 4 to 6. Makes about 1½ cups (375ml).

■ Recipe can be made a day ahead.
■ Storage: Covered, in refrigerator.
■ Freeze: Not suitable.

Also suitable for: Seafood.

BELOW: Clockwise from left: Sweet Pepper Sauce, Minted Bearnaise Sauce, Remoulade Sauce.

Below: Bowls from Home Sweet Home.

simmer, uncovered, about 10 minutes or until sauce is thickened.

Serves 6. Makes about 1 litre (4 cups).

■ Recipe can be made 3 days ahead.
■ Storage: Covered, in refrigerator.
■ Freeze: Suitable.
■ Microwave: Suitable.

Also suitable for: Pork, beef, chicken.

ABOVE: Roasted leg of lamb with, from back: Mint Jelly, Orange and Port Sauce, Mint Sauce.

Above: Plates from Royal Copenhagen; sauce ladle from The Cottage Manner.

MUSTARD HORSERADISH SAUCE

¾ cup (180ml) sour cream
1 tablespoon horseradish cream
1½ tablespoons chopped fresh mint
1 tablespoon seeded mustard

Combine all ingredients in bowl; mix well.

Serves 4. Makes about ¾ cup (180ml).

- Sauce can be made a day ahead.
- Storage: Covered, in refrigerator.
- Freeze: Not suitable.

Also suitable for: Beef.

ABOVE: From back: Greek Lemon Sauce, Mustard Horseradish Sauce.

GREEK LEMON SAUCE

40g butter
1 medium (125g) carrot, finely chopped
1 medium (150g) onion, finely chopped
1 stick celery, finely chopped
2½ cups (625ml) chicken stock
2 teaspoons cornflour
2 teaspoons water
1 egg, separated
2 tablespoons lemon juice
1 tablespoon chopped fresh dill

Heat butter in pan, add carrot, onion and celery, cook, covered, stirring occasionally, until onion is very soft. Add stock, simmer, uncovered, until reduced to 1 cup (250ml).

Strain, discard vegetables. Return liquid to pan, stir in blended cornflour and water, stir over heat until mixture boils and thickens slightly. Beat egg white in small bowl with electric mixer until soft peaks form, beat in egg yolk. Beat in juice and hot stock mixture. Return sauce to pan, whisk over heat, without boiling, until heated through. Stir in dill. Served here with lamb meatballs.

Serves 4. Makes about 1 cup (250ml).

- Recipe must be made close to serving.
- Freeze: Not suitable.
- Microwave: Not suitable.

Also suitable for: Vegetables, veal.

ROSEMARY AND ORANGE SAUCE

1 tablespoon shredded orange rind
½ cup (125ml) orange juice
2 tablespoons apricot jam, sieved
1 cup (250ml) chicken stock
60g butter, chopped
2 teaspoons cornflour
2 teaspoons water
1 tablespoon fresh rosemary leaves

Combine rind, juice, jam and stock in pan, simmer, uncovered, about 20 minutes or until reduced by half. Add butter, stir until melted. Stir in blended cornflour and water and rosemary, stir over heat until sauce boils and thickens.

Serves 4. Makes about 1 cup (250ml).

■ Sauce can be made 2 days ahead.
■ Storage: Covered, in refrigerator.
■ Freeze: Not suitable.
■ Microwave: Not suitable.
Also suitable for: Beef, pork, veal, poultry.

ONION AND MINT PUREE

80g butter
2 large (400g) onions, finely chopped
1 tablespoon chopped fresh mint

Heat butter in pan, add onions, cook, uncovered, over very low heat, stirring occasionally, about 50 minutes or until very soft but not brown. Blend or process mixture until smooth; stir in mint.

Serves 4. Makes about ½ cup (125ml).

■ Recipe can be made a day ahead.
■ Storage: Covered, in refrigerator.
■ Freeze: Not suitable.
■ Microwave: Not suitable.
Also suitable for: Duck, game.

ABOVE: From left: Rosemary and Orange Sauce, Onion and Mint Puree.

SPICY COCONUT AND ASPARAGUS SAUCE

1 cup (250ml) coconut milk
1 small fresh red chilli, finely chopped
1 clove garlic, crushed
1 tablespoon chopped roasted
   peanuts
½ cup (125ml) milk
1 tablespoon lemon juice
30g butter
1 bunch (about 250g) fresh
   asparagus, chopped
6 green shallots, chopped
1 tablespoon plain flour
¼ cup (60ml) water

Blend or process coconut milk, chilli, garlic, peanuts, milk and juice until smooth. Heat butter in pan, add asparagus and shallots, cook, stirring, until asparagus is just tender. Stir in flour, stir over heat until mixture is well combined. Remove from heat, gradually stir in milk mixture and water. Stir over heat until mixture boils and thickens. Served here with lamb chop.

Serves 4 to 6. Makes about 2½ cups (625ml).

■ Recipe best made close to serving.
■ Freeze: Not suitable.
■ Microwave: Suitable.

Also suitable for: Beef, chicken.

RED WINE AND RED PEPPER SAUCE

1 tablespoon vegetable oil
8 lamb noisettes
1½ tablespoons plain flour
⅔ cup (160ml) beef stock
¾ cup (180ml) dry red wine
¼ cup (60ml) water
½ medium (100g) red pepper, sliced

Heat oil in pan, add lamb, cook until well browned and cooked as desired. Remove from pan, keep warm. Reserve 1 tablespoon pan juices. Heat reserved juices in same pan, add flour, stir over heat until bubbling. Remove from heat, gradually stir in stock, wine, water and pepper, stir over heat until mixture boils and thickens.

Serves 4. Makes about 1¾ cups (430ml).

■ Recipe best made just before serving.
■ Freeze: Not suitable.
■ Microwave: Not suitable.

LEFT: From left: Spicy Coconut and Asparagus Sauce, Red Wine and Red Pepper Sauce.
ABOVE: From back: Lemon Caper Sauce, Vegetable and Cumin Sauce.

Left: Plates and sauceboat from Royal Copenhagen; saucepan and ladle from The Cottage Manner.

VEGETABLE AND CUMIN SAUCE

1 tablespoon vegetable oil
1 medium (150g) onion, chopped
1 medium (125g) carrot, finely chopped
200g button mushrooms, sliced
2 teaspoons cumin seeds
1 teaspoon grated fresh ginger
1 clove garlic, crushed
2 tablespoons plain flour
1¼ cups (310ml) beef stock
¼ cup (60ml) dry red wine
2 teaspoons chopped fresh rosemary

Heat oil in pan, add onion and carrot, cook, stirring, until onion is soft. Stir in mushrooms, cook, stirring, until mushrooms are soft. Stir in seeds, ginger, garlic and flour, cook, stirring, 1 minute. Remove from heat, gradually add remaining combined ingredients, stir over heat until sauce boils and thickens slightly. Served here with lamb cutlets.

Serves 4 to 6. Makes about 3 cups (750ml).

■ Recipe can be made several
   hours ahead.
■ Freeze: Not suitable.
■ Microwave: Suitable.

Also suitable for: Pork, beef.

LEMON CAPER SAUCE

40g butter
1 tablespoon plain flour
1 cup (250ml) chicken stock
¼ teaspoon grated lemon rind
¼ cup (60ml) lemon juice
¼ teaspoon sugar
2 tablespoons tiny capers
2 tablespoons chopped fresh parsley
2 tablespoons cream

Heat butter in pan, add flour, stir over heat until bubbling, remove from heat. Gradually stir in combined stock, rind, juice and sugar. Stir over heat until mixture boils and thickens; stir in capers, parsley and cream. Served here with lamb meatballs.

Serves 4. Makes about 1¼ cups (310ml).

■ Recipe can be made a day ahead.
■ Storage: Covered, in refrigerator.
■ Freeze: Not suitable.
■ Microwave: Suitable.

Also suitable for: Fish, pork, veal, chicken.

SORREL AND GINGER SAUCE

30g butter
3 green shallots, finely chopped
1 tablespoon grated fresh ginger
⅓ cup (80ml) dry white wine
¼ cup (60ml) chicken stock
300ml cream
1 bunch (75g) sorrel
125g butter, chopped

Heat butter in pan, add shallots and ginger, cook, stirring, until shallots are soft. Add wine, stock and cream, simmer, uncovered, until thickened slightly. Add sorrel, stir until just wilted. Blend sauce until smooth, adding butter gradually, blend until combined. Return sauce to pan, stir over heat, without boiling, until just heated through. Served here with lamb fillets.

Serves 4. Makes about 2 cups (500ml).

■ Recipe best made close to serving.
■ Freeze: Not suitable.
■ Microwave: Not suitable.

Also suitable for: Veal, pork, fish.

BLUEBERRY AND MINT SAUCE

4 racks lamb (3 cutlets in each)
2 tablespoons olive oil
1 teaspoon cracked black pepper
2 tablespoons chopped fresh mint
4 green shallots, chopped
1 tablespoon plain flour
⅓ cup (80ml) cassis
1 cup (250ml) beef stock
30g butter, chopped
100g fresh or frozen blueberries

Rub lamb with combined oil, pepper and mint. Place lamb in baking dish, bake in moderately hot oven about 20 minutes or until cooked as desired. Remove lamb from dish, reserve about 1 tablespoon of pan juices in dish. Add shallots, stir over heat until shallots are soft. Stir in flour, cook, stirring, until combined, remove from heat. Gradually stir in combined liqueur and stock, stir over heat until sauce boils and thickens slightly; strain. Return sauce to heat, whisk in butter, whisk over heat until butter is melted. Stir in blueberries, stir over heat until heated through. Serve sauce with lamb.

Serves 4. Makes about 1½ cups (375ml).

■ Recipe best made just before serving.
■ Freeze: Not suitable.
■ Microwave: Not suitable.

LEFT: From back: Rack of lamb with Blueberry and Mint Sauce, Sorrel and Ginger Sauce.

Front plate from Waterford Wedgwood.

CUMBERLAND SAUCE

1 medium (150g) lemon
2 medium (340g) oranges
¾ cup (180ml) redcurrant jelly
1 teaspoon Dijon mustard
2 tablespoons port
pinch ground ginger

Using a vegetable peeler, peel rind thinly from the lemon and 1 of the oranges. Cut rind into very thin strips. Place rind in small pan, cover with water, boil, uncovered, 3 minutes; drain. Squeeze juice from lemon and oranges. You need 2 tablespoons of lemon juice and ½ cup (125ml) orange juice. Combine juices, rind, jelly, mustard, port and ginger in pan, boil, uncovered, 2 minutes; cool.

Serves 4 to 6. Makes about 1½ cups (375ml).
- Recipe can be made 2 days ahead.
- Storage: Covered, in refrigerator.
- Freeze: Suitable.
- Microwave: Suitable.
Also suitable for: Pork, game.

GREEK GARLIC SAUCE

1 large (300g) potato, chopped
2 cloves garlic, crushed
½ cup (125ml) white vinegar
½ cup (125ml) light olive oil
⅓ cup (80ml) water, approximately

Boil, steam or microwave potato until tender, drain. Process potato, garlic, vinegar and oil until smooth. Add just enough water to give a pouring consistency. Served here with lamb kebabs.

Serves 6. Makes about 2 cups (500ml).
- Recipe can be made a day ahead.
- Storage: Covered, in refrigerator.
- Freeze: Not suitable.
- Microwave: Suitable.
Also suitable for: Vegetables, pork, beef.

ABOVE: From back: Greek Garlic Sauce, Cumberland Sauce.

Plates from Waterford Wedgwood.

SOUR CREAM AND DILL SAUCE

2 tablespoons vegetable oil
1 medium (150g) onion, sliced
2 cloves garlic, sliced
1.3kg boned rolled shoulder of lamb
1 cup (250ml) dry white wine
1½ cups (375ml) beef stock
½ cup (125ml) water
6 sprigs thyme
2 bay leaves
⅓ cup (80ml) sour cream
1 tablespoon chopped fresh dill
2 teaspoons cornflour
3 teaspoons water, extra

Heat half the oil in large pan, add onion and garlic, cook, stirring, until onion is soft; remove from pan. Heat remaining oil in same pan, add lamb, cook, turning, until browned all over. Add onion mixture, wine, stock, water, thyme and bay leaves to pan, simmer, covered, about 1½ hours, turning once, or until lamb is tender.

Remove lamb from pan, keep warm. Strain liquid into small pan, discard bay leaves and thyme, push solids through strainer. Simmer, uncovered, until reduced by one third. Add sour cream and dill, simmer, uncovered, 3 minutes. Stir in blended cornflour and extra water, stir over heat until sauce boils and thickens. Serve lamb with sauce.

Serves 4 to 6. Makes about 2 cups (500ml).

- Recipe best made close to serving.
- Freeze: Not suitable.
- Microwave: Not suitable.

SPICY HOI SIN SAUCE

1 bulb (70g) garlic
½ cup (125ml) hoi sin sauce
¼ cup (60ml) salt-reduced soy sauce
2 tablespoons sesame oil
1 tablespoon rice vinegar
1 tablespoon sake
1 teaspoon honey
½ teaspoon sambal oelek
2 teaspoons chopped fresh coriander

Place garlic on oven tray, bake, uncovered, in moderately hot oven, 1 hour. Cool 10 minutes, cut in half, squeeze out garlic. Blend or process garlic, sauces, oil, vinegar, sake, honey and sambal oelek, until combined. Transfer mixture to bowl; stir in coriander. Served here with lamb kebabs.

Serves 4. Makes about 1 cup (250ml).

- Sauce can be made a week ahead.
- Storage: Covered, in refrigerator.
- Freeze: Not suitable.
- Microwave: Not suitable.

Also suitable for: Beef, duck, chicken.

LEFT: From back: Shoulder of Lamb with Sour Cream and Dill Sauce, Spicy Hoi Sin Sauce.

Pottery from Kenwick Galleries.

TAMARIND DIPPING SAUCE

1 tablespoon tomato sauce
2 tablespoons soy sauce
2 tablespoons dry sherry
1 tablespoon tamarind sauce
2 teaspoons honey
1/4 cup (60ml) water

Combine all ingredients in small pan, simmer, uncovered, 2 minutes. Serve hot. Served here with lamb meatballs.

Serves 8. Makes 2/3 cup (160ml).

▓ Recipe can be made a day ahead.
▓ Storage: Covered, in refrigerator.
▓ Freeze: Not suitable.
▓ Microwave: Suitable.

Also suitable for: Beef, pork.

SLIMMERS' MINTED LEMON SAUCE

2 teaspoons butter
1/4 cup (60ml) lemon juice
1 tablespoon chopped fresh mint

Combine all ingredients in pan, stir over heat until mixture boils. Served here with char-grilled lamb leg steaks.

Serves 4. Makes about 1/3 cup (80ml).

▓ Recipe best made just before serving.
▓ Freeze: Not suitable.
▓ Microwave: Suitable.

Also suitable for: Vegetables, chicken, seafood, veal.

CREAMY PESTO SAUCE

1 cup firmly packed fresh basil leaves
2 cloves garlic, crushed
1/3 cup (50g) pine nuts, toasted
3 teaspoons olive oil
1/4 cup (20g) grated parmesan cheese
1 cup (250ml) cream

Process basil, garlic, nuts, oil and cheese until smooth. Combine basil mixture and cream in pan, simmer, uncovered, 3 minutes. Served here with sliced lamb fillet.

Serves 6. Makes about 2 cups (500ml).

▓ Sauce can be made a day ahead.
▓ Storage: Cover surface with plastic wrap, store in refrigerator.
▓ Freeze: Not suitable.
▓ Microwave: Suitable.

Also suitable for: Beef, veal, chicken, pasta.

LAMB GRAVY

2 teaspoons vegetable oil
1.5kg shoulder of lamb
1 medium (150g) onion, chopped
1 medium (125g) carrot, chopped
1 stick celery, chopped
2 sprigs fresh thyme
2 tablespoons dry red wine
2 tablespoons water
1/4 cup (35g) plain flour
2 cups (500ml) water, extra
2 teaspoons redcurrant jelly
2 teaspoons chicken stock powder

Heat oil in baking dish, add lamb, cook over high heat until browned all over; remove lamb from dish. Add onion, carrot and celery to dish, cook, stirring, 3 minutes. Return lamb to dish, add thyme, wine and water. Bake, uncovered, in moderately hot oven about 1 hour or until lamb is cooked as desired.

Remove lamb from dish; reserve pan juices. Place baking dish over heat, add flour, cook, stirring, until well browned. Remove dish from heat, add extra water, jelly and stock powder, stir until combined. Stir over heat until sauce boils and thickens, simmer, uncovered, 2 minutes. Push mixture through coarse sieve.

Serves 4. Makes about 1 cup (250ml).

▓ Recipe best made close to serving.
▓ Freeze: Suitable.
▓ Microwave: Not suitable.

BELOW: From back: Creamy Pesto Sauce, Lamb Gravy.

Pottery from Kenwick Galleries.

LEFT: From back: Slimmers' Minted Lemon Sauce, Tamarind Dipping Sauce.

Plates and tray from Home Sweet Home.

APRICOT SAUCE

1 tablespoon light olive oil
1 medium (150g) onion,
    finely chopped
1 teaspoon chopped fresh thyme
1 cup (about 250g) undrained
    canned pie apricots
1 cup (250ml) chicken stock
¼ cup (60ml) dry white wine
½ teaspoon sugar

Heat oil in pan, add onion and thyme, cook, stirring, until onion is soft. Add apricots and remaining ingredients to pan, simmer, uncovered, stirring occasionally, about 5 minutes or until sauce is slightly reduced. Blend or process apricot mixture until smooth. Served here with lamb kebabs.

Serves 4. Makes about 2 cups (500ml).

- Sauce can be made a day ahead.
- Storage: Covered, in refrigerator.
- Freeze: Not suitable.
- Microwave: Not suitable.

Also suitable for: Chicken, pork.

CREAMY MADEIRA SAUCE

30g butter
¼ cup (60ml) Madeira
1½ tablespoons chopped
    fresh tarragon
300ml cream
1 teaspoon cornflour
2 teaspoons water

Heat butter in pan, stir in Madeira. Stir in tarragon and cream, bring to boil, stir in blended cornflour and water, stir over heat until sauce boils and thickens.

Serves 4. Makes about 1½ cups (375ml).

- Recipe best made close to serving.
- Freeze: Not suitable.
- Microwave: Suitable.

Also suitable for: Beef, chicken.

LEFT: From left: Apricot Sauce, Creamy Madeira Sauce.

Plates from Villeroy & Boch.

for pork & veal

Pork and veal often feature as special occasion meats. For celebrations, try one of the sauces starring distinctive or unusual ingredients.

BLACK BEAN SAUCE

2 tablespoons vegetable oil
2 cloves garlic, crushed
⅓ cup (65g) canned black beans, rinsed, drained
1 tablespoon grated fresh ginger
3 teaspoons cornflour
1½ cups (375ml) water

Heat oil in pan, add garlic, black beans and ginger, cook, stirring, 5 minutes. Stir in blended cornflour and water, stir over heat until sauce boils and thickens. Blend or process sauce until smooth. Return to pan, simmer, uncovered, until slightly thickened. Served here with meatballs.

Serves 4. Makes about 1⅓ cups (330ml).

■ Recipe best made close to serving.
■ Freeze: Suitable.
■ Microwave: Not suitable.

Also suitable for: Beef, chicken, fish.

CALVADOS AND APPLE SAUCE

1 tablespoon vegetable oil
20g butter
4 French shallots, finely chopped
1 medium (120g) carrot, chopped
1 stick celery, finely chopped
½ cup (125ml) Calvados
1 cup (250ml) dry cider
6 parsley stems
1½ cups (375ml) chicken stock
⅔ cup (160ml) cream
2 teaspoons cornflour
1 tablespoon water

GLAZED APPLES
20g butter
2 teaspoons sugar
1 medium (150g) apple, peeled, sliced

Heat oil and butter in pan, add shallots, carrot and celery, cook, stirring, until shallots are very soft. Add half the Calvados, simmer, uncovered, until nearly all liquid is evaporated. Add cider and parsley, simmer, uncovered, until reduced by half. Add stock, simmer, uncovered until reduced by half. Stir in cream, blended cornflour and water, stir over heat until mixture boils and thickens. Stir in remaining Calvados; strain. Serve with glazed apples.
Glazed Apples: Heat butter in pan, add sugar and apple, cook, turning until apple is tender and browned.

Serves 4. Makes about 2 cups (500ml).

■ Sauce can be made a day ahead, apples best made close to serving.
■ Storage: Covered, in refrigerator.
■ Freeze: Not suitable.
■ Microwave: Not suitable.

Also suitable for: Chicken.

LEFT: From back: Calvados and Apple Sauce, Black Bean Sauce.

SOUR CREAM AND PAPRIKA SAUCE

20g butter
½ small (40g) onion, chopped
1 clove garlic, crushed
½ small (75g) green pepper, chopped
70g button mushrooms, sliced
2 teaspoons plain flour
1 teaspoon paprika
½ teaspoon Worcestershire sauce
1 teaspoon lemon juice
2 teaspoons tomato paste
½ cup (125ml) chicken stock
⅓ cup (80ml) sour cream

Heat butter in pan, add onion, garlic and pepper, cook, stirring, until onion is soft. Add mushrooms, cook, stirring, until mushrooms are tender. Add flour and paprika, stir until well combined. Gradually stir in combined Worcestershire sauce, juice, paste and stock, simmer, uncovered, 5 minutes. Add sour cream, stir until heated through. Served here with pork fillet slices.

Serves 4. Makes about 1⅓ cups (330ml).

- Recipe best made just before serving.
- Freeze: Not suitable.
- Microwave: Suitable.

Also suitable for: Chicken, beef.

MANGO SAUCE

½ cup (100g) chopped fresh mango
½ cup (125ml) cream
¼ cup (60ml) dry white wine
1 tablespoon chopped hazelnuts
pinch cayenne pepper
2 teaspoons French mustard
1 tablespoon chopped fresh chives

Blend or process mango until smooth. Combine mango puree, cream, wine, nuts, pepper and mustard in pan, stir over heat until heated through. Stir in chives. Served here with veal loin steaks.

Serves 4. Makes about 1 cup (250ml).

- Recipe can be made a day ahead.
- Storage: Covered, in refrigerator.
- Freeze: Not suitable.
- Microwave: Suitable.

Also suitable for: Chicken, seafood.

EGG AND ANCHOVY BUTTER

1 hard-boiled egg
3 drained anchovy fillets, chopped
125g soft butter
2 teaspoons lemon juice
½ teaspoon cracked black peppercorns
1 tablespoon finely chopped red pepper
3 teaspoons chopped fresh chives
3 teaspoons chopped fresh parsley

Process egg, anchovies, butter, juice and peppercorns until smooth. Transfer mixture to bowl, stir in pepper and herbs; mix well. Spoon mixture onto sheet of foil, roll up into log shape, twisting ends; freeze until firm. Served here with crumbed veal.

Serves 8.

- Recipe can be made 2 days ahead.
- Storage: Covered, in refrigerator.
- Freeze: Suitable.

Also suitable for: Chicken, seafood, vegetables.

CORIANDER SAUCE

3 teaspoons cornflour
1¼ cups (310ml) water
2 teaspoon grated fresh ginger
1 tablespoon chopped fresh coriander
½ small fresh red chilli, chopped
1 clove garlic, crushed
2 teaspoons sugar
1 teaspoon chicken stock powder
1 teaspoon grated lime rind
1 teaspoon lime juice
2 teaspoons soy sauce
2 teaspoons fish sauce

Blend cornflour and water in pan, stir in remaining ingredients; stir over heat until sauce boils and thickens. Served here with meatballs.

Serves 4. Makes about 1¼ cups (310ml).

- Recipe best made just before serving.
- Freeze: Not suitable.
- Microwave: Suitable.

BELOW: From back: Coriander Sauce, Egg and Anchovy Butter.

China from Royal Copenhagen; tray from Accoutrement.

LEFT: From left: Mango Sauce, Sour Cream and Paprika Sauce.

China from Villeroy & Boch.

PIMIENTO AND OLIVE SAUCE

1 tablespoon olive oil
1 medium (150g) onion,
 finely chopped
1 clove garlic, crushed
1 teaspoon chopped fresh thyme
½ teaspoon chopped fresh rosemary
¼ cup (35g) chopped drained
 sun-dried tomatoes
1 medium (130g) tomato, chopped
2 x 390g cans red pimientos, drained
1 tablespoon chopped seedless
 black olives
1 tablespoon water, approximately

Heat oil in pan, add onion, garlic and herbs; cook, stirring, until onion is soft. Blend or process onion mixture, sun-dried tomatoes, tomato and pimientos until smooth, strain puree into bowl. Stir in olives and enough water to make a thick sauce. Served here with pork kebabs.

Serves 6. Makes 2¼ cups (560ml).

■ Sauce can be made a day ahead.
■ Storage: Covered, in refrigerator.
■ Freeze: Suitable.
■ Microwave: Suitable.

Also suitable for: Chicken, fish.

LEMON PEPPER GLAZE

2 tablespoons honey
½ cup (125ml) water
½ teaspoon chicken stock powder
1 teaspoon lemon pepper
2 teaspoons cornflour
¼ cup (60ml) lemon juice
1 medium (180g) orange, segmented
2 green shallots, chopped

Combine honey, water, stock powder and pepper in pan; stir in blended cornflour and juice; stir over heat until glaze boils and thickens, stir in orange and shallots. Served here with pork fillets.

Serves 6. Makes about 1¼ cups (310ml).

CHEESY CURRY SAUCE

30g butter
1 teaspoon curry powder
1 tablespoon plain flour
1 cup (250ml) milk
½ cup (60g) grated tasty
cheddar cheese

Melt butter in pan, stir in curry powder and flour, stir over heat 1 minute. Remove from heat, gradually stir in milk, stir constantly over heat until sauce boils and thickens. Remove pan from heat, add cheese, stir until melted. Served here with pork sausages.

Serves 6. Makes about 1¼ cups (310ml).

■ Sauce best made just before serving.
■ Freeze: Not suitable.
■ Microwave: Suitable.

Also suitable for: Vegetables.

MUSHROOM AND GARLIC SAUCE

1 bulb garlic
40g butter
200g button mushrooms, quartered
¼ cup (60ml) sweet sherry
4 green shallots, sliced
2 teaspoons cornflour
⅔ cup (160ml) chicken stock

Place garlic on oven tray, bake, uncovered, in moderately hot oven 1 hour. Cool 10 minutes, cut in half horizontally, squeeze out garlic. Heat butter in pan, add garlic and mushrooms, cook, stirring, until mushrooms are tender. Add sherry, simmer, uncovered, until reduced by half. Add shallots and blended cornflour and stock, stir over heat until sauce boils and thickens. Served here with pork chops.

Serves 4. Makes about 2 cups (500ml).

■ Sauce can be made a day ahead.
■ Storage: Covered, in refrigerator.
■ Freeze: Suitable.
■ Microwave: Not suitable.

Also suitable for: Beef, lamb, vegetables.

■ Glaze best made just before serving.
■ Freeze: Not suitable.
■ Microwave: Suitable.

Also suitable for: Chicken.

ABOVE: From left: Pimiento and Olive Sauce, Lemon Pepper Glaze.

ABOVE: From left: Cheesy Curry Sauce, Mushroom and Garlic Sauce.

Right hand plate from Villeroy & Boch.

LEEK AND TOMATO SAUCE

30g butter
2 large (1kg) leeks, sliced
1 medium (130g) tomato,
**   peeled, chopped**
300g can Tomato Supreme
½ teaspoon sugar
1 tablespoon chopped fresh chives
½ cup (50g) grated mozzarella
**   cheese**

Heat butter in pan, add leeks and tomato, cook, stirring, until leeks are soft. Add Tomato Supreme, sugar and chives, stir until heated through. Serve sauce sprinkled with cheese.

Serves 6. Makes about 3½ cups (875ml).

■ Recipe can be made a day ahead.
■ Storage: Covered, in refrigerator.
■ Freeze: Not suitable.
■ Microwave: Suitable.

Also suitable for: Lamb, chicken, fish.

FRUITY PROSCIUTTO SAUCE

100g sliced prosciutto
2 tablespoons vegetable oil
2 medium (300g) onions, sliced
1 large (200g) apple, peeled, sliced
¼ teaspoon five spice powder
1 tablespoon teriyaki sauce
1½ cups (375ml) orange juice
1 tablespoon chopped fresh
**   rosemary**

Cut prosciutto into thin strips. Heat oil in pan, add onions and apple, cook, stirring, until onions are soft. Add prosciutto, five spice powder, teriyaki sauce and juice, simmer, uncovered, about 2 minutes or until apple is soft; stir in rosemary.

Serves 4. Makes about 2¼ cups (560ml).

■ Recipe can be made a day ahead.
■ Storage: Covered, in refrigerator.
■ Freeze: Not suitable.
■ Microwave: Not suitable.

Also suitable for: Chicken.

SPICY APRICOT SAUCE

425g can apricot nectar
¼ cup (60ml) white wine vinegar
2 teaspoons soy sauce
1 tablespoon mild sweet chilli sauce
1 clove garlic, crushed
2 teaspoons grated fresh ginger
2 teaspoons cornflour
1 tablespoon water

Combine nectar, vinegar, soy and chilli sauces, garlic, ginger, blended cornflour and water in pan, simmer, uncovered, stirring occasionally, about 15 minutes or until sauce is reduced and thickened.

Serves 4. Makes about 1¾ cups (430ml).

■ Sauce can be made a day ahead.
■ Storage: Covered, in refrigerator.
■ Freeze: Not suitable.
■ Microwave: Suitable.

Also suitable for: Chicken.

BELOW: Clockwise from top left: Leek and Tomato Sauce, Fruity Prosciutto Sauce, Spicy Apricot Sauce.

Below: China, trivets, whisks and ladles from Accoutrement.

MUSTARD AND SHERRY SAUCE

1 tablespoon vegetable oil
4 large veal chops
2 tablespoons dry sherry
1 clove garlic, crushed
2 teaspoons Dijon mustard
1 teaspoon seeded mustard
1½ cups (375ml) beef stock
1 tablespoon cornflour
1 tablespoon water
1 tablespoon chopped fresh dill
1 teaspoon dry sherry, extra

Heat oil in pan, add chops, cook until tender; drain on absorbent paper. Add sherry and garlic to same pan, simmer, uncovered, 1 minute. Add mustards and stock, simmer, uncovered, 3 minutes, add blended cornflour and water; stir over heat until mixture boils and thickens. Stir in dill and extra sherry. Serve sauce over veal chops.

Serves 4. Makes about 1 cup (250ml).

■ Recipe best made just before serving.
■ Freeze: Not suitable.
■ Microwave: Not suitable.

ABOVE: From left: Tandoori Mango Sauce, Mustard and Sherry Sauce.

TANDOORI MANGO SAUCE

400ml can coconut milk
425g can mango halves, drained
1 tablespoon bottled tandoori paste
½ teaspoon sambal oelek
2 cloves garlic, crushed
1 cup (250ml) vegetable stock

Blend or process milk, mangoes, paste, sambal oelek, garlic and stock until smooth. Transfer mixture to pan, stir over heat until heated through.

Serves 6. Makes about 3½ cups (875ml).

■ Recipe can be made a day ahead.
■ Storage: Covered, in refrigerator.
■ Freeze: Not suitable.
■ Microwave: Suitable.

Also suitable for: Chicken.

SWEET AND SOUR LYCHEE SAUCE

1 tablespoon vegetable oil
1 medium (150g) onion, sliced
1 clove garlic, crushed
1 medium (200g) red pepper, chopped
1 tablespoon cornflour
1 cup (250ml) pineapple juice
1 cup (250ml) water
2 teaspoons white vinegar
2 tablespoons hoi sin sauce
425g can lychees, drained, halved

Heat oil in pan, add onion, garlic and pepper, cook, stirring, until onion is soft. Stir in blended cornflour and juice, water, vinegar and hoi sin sauce, cook, stirring, until mixture boils and thickens, add lychees, stir until heated through. Served here with pork strips.

Serves 6. Makes about 3½ cups (875ml).

■ Recipe can be made 2 hours ahead.
■ Storage: Covered, in refrigerator.
■ Freeze: Not suitable.
■ Microwave: Not suitable.

Also suitable for: Chicken.

WHITE WINE AND ROSEMARY SAUCE

20g butter
1 green shallot, finely chopped
½ medium (120g) carrot, finely chopped
½ stick celery, finely chopped
1 tablespoon fresh rosemary leaves
1 teaspoon plain flour
1 cup (250ml) chicken stock
½ cup (125ml) dry white wine

Heat butter in small pan, add vegetables and rosemary, cook, stirring, until soft. Add flour, cook, stirring, about 1 minute or until mixture is dry and grainy. Gradually add stock and wine, simmer about 5 minutes or until thickened slightly. Served here with sliced pork.

Serves 6. Makes about 1¼ cups (310ml).

■ Sauce best made on day of serving.
■ Storage: Covered, in refrigerator.
■ Freeze: Suitable.
■ Microwave: Suitable.

APPLE CREAM

1 medium (150g) apple, peeled
½ cup (125ml) cream, lightly whipped
½ cup (125ml) sour cream
¼ teaspoon grated lemon rind
1 tablespoon lemon juice
1 tablespoon chopped fresh parsley
1 tablespoon drained chopped capers
1 green shallot, finely chopped

Cut apple into thin strips. Combine creams, rind, juice, parsley, capers and shallots in bowl, fold in apple. Served here with pork steak.

Serves 4. Makes about 1¼ cups (310ml).

■ Recipe best made close to serving.
■ Freeze: Not suitable.

HERB AND LEMON SAUCE

1 tablespoon vegetable oil
4 veal steaks
1 tablespoon lemon juice
2 cloves garlic, crushed
1 cup (250ml) cream
1 tablespoon chopped fresh chives
1 teaspoon chopped fresh oregano
1 teaspoon chopped fresh thyme
½ teaspoon grated lemon rind

Heat oil in pan, add veal, cook until tender, remove from pan. Add juice and garlic to same pan, cook, stirring, 1 minute; add cream, simmer, uncovered, about 4 minutes or until thickened slightly, add herbs and rind, stir until heated through. Serve sauce over veal.

Serves 4. Makes about ¾ cup (180ml).

■ Recipe best made just before serving.
■ Freeze: Not suitable.
■ Microwave: Not suitable.

Also suitable for: Chicken.

LEFT: From left: Herb and Lemon Sauce, Apple Cream.
ABOVE: From left: Sweet and Sour Lychee Sauce, White Wine and Rosemary Sauce.

Above: Bowls and jug from Home & Garden on the Mall.

APPLE SAUCE

**3 medium (450g) apples,
    peeled, chopped
2 tablespoons water
2½ tablespoons sugar
½ teaspoon mixed spice
1 teaspoon butter**

Combine apples and water in pan, simmer, covered, stirring occasionally, about 8 minutes or until apples are soft. Stir in sugar, spice and butter, beat with wooden spoon until smooth.

Serves 6. Makes about 1½ cups (375ml).

- ■ Sauce can be made 3 days ahead.
- ■ Storage: Covered, in refrigerator.
- ■ Freeze: Suitable.
- ■ Microwave: Not suitable.

Also suitable for: Game.

PRUNE AND RED WINE SAUCE

**⅔ cup (110g) seedless prunes, halved
1 cup (250ml) dry red wine
1.5kg boned rolled loin of pork
1 tablespoon vegetable oil
1 teaspoon salt
2 tablespoons plain flour
1½ cups (375ml) beef stock
1 tablespoon chopped fresh sage**

Combine prunes and wine in bowl, cover, stand 3 hours or overnight. Rub pork rind with oil and salt. Place pork on wire rack over baking dish, bake, uncovered, in hot oven about 10 minutes or until rind begins to crackle. Reduce heat to moderate, bake further 1¼ hours or until pork is tender. Remove pork from baking dish. Drain prunes, reserve wine. Discard all but 2 tablespoons juice from dish, stir flour into dish, stir over heat until bubbling. Remove from heat, gradually stir in ½ cup (125ml) of the reserved wine and the stock, stir over heat until sauce boils and thickens. Strain sauce into pan, add prunes, sage and further 1 tablespoon of reserved wine, simmer, uncovered, 2 minutes.

Serves 6 to 8. Makes about 2 cups (500ml).

- ■ Recipe best made close to serving.
- ■ Freeze: Not suitable.
- ■ Microwave: Not suitable.

PEAR AND GINGER SAUCE

**1 tablespoon light olive oil
1 small (80g) onion, chopped
1 tablespoon grated fresh ginger
1 clove garlic, crushed
2 tablespoons dry white wine
1¾ cups (430ml) chicken stock
125g dried pears, chopped
2 teaspoons chopped fresh thyme
1 teaspoon lemon juice**

Heat oil in pan, add onion, ginger and garlic, cook, stirring, until onion is soft. Add wine, simmer, uncovered, until almost all liquid is evaporated. Stir in stock, pears, thyme and juice, simmer, covered, about 10 minutes or until pears are soft. Blend or process sauce until smooth.

Serves 6. Makes about 2 cups (500ml).

- ■ Sauce can be made 2 days ahead.
- ■ Storage: Covered, in refrigerator.
- ■ Freeze: Suitable.
- ■ Microwave: Suitable.

Also suitable for: Chicken.

RAISIN AND CELERY SAUCE

**⅓ cup (55g) raisins
½ cup (125ml) dry white wine
40g butter
1 stick celery, finely sliced
1 tablespoon plain flour
1 cup (250ml) vegetable stock
2 tablespoons cream**

Combine raisins and wine in bowl, stand 20 minutes. Strain raisins, reserve wine. Heat butter in pan, add celery, cook, stirring, until just soft. Add flour, cook, stirring, until combined. Remove pan from heat, gradually stir in wine, stock and raisins. Stir over heat until mixture boils and thickens. Remove from heat, stir in cream.

Serves 6. Makes about 2 cups (500ml).

- ■ Sauce best made just before serving.
- ■ Freeze: Not suitable.
- ■ Microwave: Suitable.

TOMATO SPINACH SAUCE

**410g can tomatoes
1 tablespoon tomato paste
1 tablespoon light olive oil
1 medium (150g) onion, chopped
1 clove garlic, crushed
1 teaspoon sugar
¼ cup (60ml) dry white wine
¼ cup (60ml) water
½ bunch (about 325g) English
    spinach, shredded**

Blend or process tomatoes and paste until smooth. Heat oil in pan, add onion and garlic, cook, stirring, until onion is soft. Add tomato mixture, sugar, wine and water, simmer, uncovered, 5 minutes. Stir in spinach, cook, stirring, about 3 minutes or until spinach is just wilted.

Serves 4. Makes about 2½ cups (625ml).

- ■ Recipe best made just before serving.
- ■ Freeze: Not suitable.
- ■ Microwave: Suitable.

Also suitable for: Fish, chicken.

*BELOW: Roast loin of pork served with Prune and Red Wine Sauce and Apple Sauce.
RIGHT: Clockwise from left: Raisin and Celery Sauce, Pear and Ginger Sauce, Tomato Spinach Sauce.*

*Right: Bowls and saucepan from Accoutrement.
Below: Plate and bowl from Accoutrement.*

MUSTARD AND VEGETABLE SAUCE

2 tablespoons olive oil
1 rack of veal (8 cutlets)
2 tablespoons chopped fresh oregano
2 cloves garlic, crushed
½ medium (100g) red pepper, finely chopped
½ small leek, finely chopped
75g green beans, finely chopped
½ stick celery, finely chopped
½ medium (120g) carrot, finely chopped
¼ cup (60ml) dry red wine
⅓ cup (80ml) beef stock
300ml cream
2 tablespoons seeded mustard
2 teaspoons Dijon mustard
1 tablespoon chopped fresh parsley

Heat half the oil in baking dish, add veal, cook until well browned. Spread veal with combined oregano, garlic and remaining oil. Bake, uncovered, in moderate oven about 40 minutes or until cooked as desired. Remove veal from pan. Remove any burnt pieces from pan, add vegetables, cook, stirring, until almost tender. Stir in wine, stock and cream, simmer, uncovered, about 5 minutes or until slightly thickened. Stir in mustards and parsley, simmer further 2 minutes. Serve sauce with veal.

Serves 4. Makes about 2½ cups (625ml).

- Recipe best made close to serving.
- Freeze: Not suitable.
- Microwave: Not suitable.

BELOW: From left: Orange Maple Sauce, Mustard and Vegetable Sauce.
RIGHT: From left: Roasted Pepita Salsa, Dill Pickle Sauce.

Below: China from Villeroy & Boch.

ORANGE MAPLE SAUCE

1 tablespoon vegetable oil
1 medium (150g) onion, finely chopped
2 teaspoons grated orange rind
½ cup (125ml) orange juice
¼ cup (60ml) maple syrup
½ teaspoon chopped fresh rosemary
2 teaspoons cornflour
¼ cup (60ml) water
1 teaspoon chopped fresh mint

Heat oil in pan, add onion, cook, stirring, until onion is very soft. Add rind, juice, syrup, rosemary and blended cornflour and water, stir over heat until mixture boils and thickens. Stir in mint. Served here with pork chops.

Serves 4. Makes about 1⅓ cups (330ml).

- Sauce can be made a day ahead.
- Storage: Covered, in refrigerator.
- Freeze: Suitable.
- Microwave: Suitable.

ROASTED PEPITA SALSA

1 teaspoon vegetable oil
¾ cup (110g) pepitas
¼ teaspoon ground cumin
1 medium (130g) tomato, peeled
1 clove garlic, crushed
1 tablespoon lime juice
**2 tablespoons chopped
    fresh coriander**
**1½ tablespoons chopped
    fresh chives**
**1 bottled jalapeno pepper,
    drained, seeded**
¼ cup (60ml) chicken stock

Heat oil in pan, add pepitas, cook, stirring, until browned and crisp; pepitas will pop during cooking. Add cumin, stir over heat until fragrant. Process pepita mixture until fine, transfer to bowl. Process tomato and remaining ingredients until smooth. Combine pepitas and tomato mixture in bowl. Served here with barbecued pork leg steaks.

Serves 4 to 6. Makes about 1½ cups (375ml).

■ Recipe can be made a week ahead.
■ Storage: Covered, in refrigerator.
■ Freeze: Not suitable.
■ Microwave: Not Suitable.

Also suitable for: Beef, lamb, chicken.

DILL PICKLE SAUCE

1kg nut of veal
1 tablespoon vegetable oil
¼ cup (60ml) dry white wine
30g butter
½ small (40g) onion, finely chopped
1 teaspoon white wine vinegar
1 tablespoon plain flour
1 cup (250ml) beef stock
**1 tablespoon finely chopped
    dill pickle**
2 tablespoons water
½ teaspoon French mustard

Place veal on wire rack over a baking dish, brush with oil. Bake in moderate oven about 1½ hours or until cooked as desired. Remove veal from dish, stand, covered, 10 minutes, reserve juices in dish. Place dish on top of stove, stir in wine, simmer until reduced by half. Add butter and onion to dish, cook, stirring, until onion is soft, add vinegar and flour, cook, stirring, 3 minutes, remove from heat. Gradually stir in stock, return to heat, simmer, uncovered, 2 minutes, add dill pickle, water and mustard, simmer 2 minutes. Serve with sliced meat.

Serves 4. Makes about 1 cup (250ml).

■ Sauce best made just before serving.
■ Freeze: Not suitable.
■ Microwave: Not suitable.

BRANDIED GINGER PLUM SAUCE

1 small (80g) onion, finely chopped
1 teaspoon grated fresh ginger
1 clove garlic, crushed
¼ cup (60ml) water
2 drained canned plums, seeded
¼ cup (60ml) syrup from
canned plums
3 teaspoons brandy

Combine onion, ginger, garlic and water in pan, cook, stirring, until onion is soft. Add plums, syrup and brandy, bring to the boil, simmer, uncovered, 1 minute. Blend or process sauce until smooth, return to pan, stir over heat until hot. Served here with pork ribs.

Serves 4. Makes about 1 cup (250ml).

■ Recipe can be made a day ahead.
■ Storage: Covered, in refrigerator.
■ Freeze: Suitable.
■ Microwave: Suitable.

Also suitable for: Quail, duck.

PEANUT LIME DIPPING SAUCE

⅓ cup (50g) roasted unsalted peanuts
¾ cup (180ml) white vinegar
¾ cup (165g) sugar
2 teaspoons grated fresh ginger
2 teaspoons grated lime rind
2 tablespoons lime juice
1 small fresh red chilli, finely chopped
2 tablespoons chopped fresh
lemon grass
3 teaspoons fish sauce
1 tablespoon chopped fresh mint
1 tablespoon chopped
fresh coriander

Process peanuts until finely minced. Combine vinegar, sugar, ginger, rind, juice, chilli and lemon grass in small pan, stir over heat until sugar is dissolved. Simmer, uncovered, 5 minutes, stir in sauce and peanuts. Cool mixture, stir in herbs. Served here with pork kebabs.

Serves 6. Makes about 1½ cups (375ml).

■ Sauce can be made a day ahead. Add herbs just before serving.
■ Storage: Covered, in refrigerator.
■ Freeze: Not suitable.
■ Microwave: Not suitable.

Also suitable for: Beef, chicken, lamb.

TOMATILLO SAUCE

510g can tomatillos, drained
4 small fresh green chillies, seeded,
finely chopped
1 clove garlic, crushed
2 tablespoons chopped fresh
coriander
½ small (40g) onion, finely chopped

Process tomatillos, chillies, garlic, coriander and onion until combined (do not overprocess, mixture should be chunky). Transfer mixture to bowl. Served here with pork burgers.

Serves 4. Makes about 1½ cups (375ml).

■ Recipe can be made a day ahead.
■ Storage: Covered, in refrigerator.
■ Freeze: Not suitable.

Also suitable for: Chicken, lamb, beef.

LEFT: Clockwise from left: Tomatillo Sauce, Brandied Ginger Plum Sauce, Peanut Lime Dipping Sauce.

China from Portmeirion.

for vegetables & salads

These tempting sauces will not only add savour to cooked vegetables and salads, but will also combine wonderfully with meat, poultry and seafood.

BLUE CHEESE SAUCE

30g butter
1 clove garlic, crushed
1 medium (about 150g) onion, chopped
125g blue cheese, crumbled
1 tablespoon cornflour
½ cup (125ml) cream
½ cup (125ml) milk
1 teaspoon grated lemon rind
1 teaspoon lemon juice

Heat butter in pan, add garlic and onion, cook, stirring, until onion is soft. Add cheese, cook, stirring, until melted. Stir in blended cornflour and cream, then milk, cook, stirring, until mixture boils and thickens, stir in rind and juice.

Serves 6. Makes about 2 cups (500ml).

■ Recipe best made just before serving.
■ Freeze: Not suitable.
■ Microwave: Not suitable.

Also suitable for: Beef.

NUTTY RED AND YELLOW PEPPER SAUCE

2 medium (400g) red peppers
2 medium (400g) yellow peppers
¼ cup (35g) chopped macadamias, toasted
½ teaspoon sambal oelek
2 tablespoons lemon juice
½ cup (125ml) olive oil

Quarter peppers, remove seeds and membrane. Grill peppers, skin side up, until skin blisters and blackens. Peel away skin, chop peppers. Blend or process red peppers with half the nuts, half the sambal oelek, half the juice and half the oil until smooth. Repeat with yellow peppers and remaining ingredients.

Serves 4. Makes about 1 cup (250ml) of each sauce.

■ Recipe can be made a day ahead.
■ Storage: Covered, in refrigerator.
■ Freeze: Not suitable.
■ Microwave: Not suitable.

Also suitable for: Chicken, fish.

MINTED COCONUT SAUCE

1 tablespoon vegetable oil
1 medium (150g) onion, chopped
1 clove garlic, crushed
1 small fresh red chilli, seeded, chopped
1 tablespoon curry powder
2 teaspoons lemon juice
½ cup (125ml) cream
1 cup (250ml) coconut cream
2 tablespoons chopped fresh coriander
1 tablespoon chopped fresh mint

Heat oil in pan, add onion, garlic, chilli and curry powder; cook, stirring, until onion is soft. Stir in juice and creams, simmer, uncovered, about 5 minutes or until thickened. Stir in herbs.

Serves 6. Makes about 1¾ cups (430ml).

■ Recipe can be made 2 hours ahead.
■ Storage: Covered, in refrigerator.
■ Freeze: Not suitable.
■ Microwave: Not suitable.

Also suitable for: Chicken, fish.

RIGHT: Clockwise from top right, Nutty Red and Yellow Pepper Sauce, Blue Cheese Sauce, Minted Coconut Sauce.

SPICY AVOCADO SAUCE

2 teaspoons light olive oil
1 clove garlic, crushed
1 teaspoon grated fresh ginger
½ teaspoon ground cumin
½ teaspoon ground coriander
½ teaspoon five spice powder
½ cup (125ml) coconut milk
1 medium (250g) avocado, chopped
1 tablespoon milk

Heat oil in pan, add garlic, ginger and spices; cook, stirring, until fragrant; add coconut milk. Blend or process coconut mixture, avocado and milk until smooth.

Serves 4. Makes about 1 cup (250ml).

■ Recipe best made just before serving.
■ Freeze: Not suitable.
■ Microwave: Not suitable.

Also suitable for: Seafood.

BELOW: From left: Spicy Avocado Sauce, Red Lentil Sauce, Lemon and Ginger Sauce.

LEMON AND GINGER SAUCE

2 cups (500ml) chicken stock
5cm piece lemon rind
⅔ cup (160ml) lemon juice
5cm (40g) piece ginger, peeled, thinly sliced
⅓ cup (65g) brown sugar, firmly packed
1½ tablespoons cornflour
2 tablespoons water
6 green shallots, finely chopped

Combine stock, rind, juice, ginger and sugar in pan, simmer, uncovered, 5 minutes. Strain sauce, return to pan, add blended cornflour and water, stir until sauce boils and thickens; reduce heat, simmer 5 minutes. Stir in shallots.

Serves 6. Makes about 3 cups (750ml).

■ Sauce best made just before serving.
■ Freeze: Not suitable.
■ Microwave: Suitable.

Also suitable for: Chicken, seafood.

RED LENTIL SAUCE

¼ cup (50g) red lentils
½ teaspoon grated fresh ginger
1 tablespoon brown sugar
¼ cup (60ml) white wine vinegar
¼ cup (60ml) orange juice
2 teaspoons Dijon mustard
½ cup (125ml) olive oil

Add lentils to pan of boiling water, boil, uncovered, about 8 minutes or until tender, drain.Combine lentils, ginger, sugar, vinegar, juice and mustard in pan, stir over heat until sugar is dissolved, add oil, stir until heated through.

Serves 6. Makes about 1½ cups (375ml).

■ Sauce can be made a day ahead.
■ Storage: Covered, in refrigerator.
■ Freeze: Suitable.
■ Microwave: Suitable.

Also suitable for: Chicken, pork.

RIGHT: Clockwise from top: Anchovy Hollandaise, Warm Peppercorn Sauce, Sour Cream Sauce.

ANCHOVY HOLLANDAISE

4 egg yolks
2 tablespoons lemon juice
2 tablespoons water
250g butter, melted
2 canned drained anchovy fillets,
  finely chopped
1 tablespoon chopped fresh basil

Beat combined egg yolks, juice and water in heatproof bowl over pan of simmering water until thick, remove from heat. Gradually whisk in hot butter in a thin, steady stream; discard white residue. Stir in anchovies and basil.

Serves 6. Makes about 1½ cups (375ml).

■ Recipe best made close to serving.
■ Freeze: Not suitable.
■ Microwave: Not suitable.
Also suitable for: Beef.

WARM PEPPERCORN SAUCE

20g butter
1 small (80g) onion, chopped
2 tablespoons brandy
2 teaspoons drained green
  peppercorns
⅓ cup (80ml) sour cream
¼ cup (60ml) milk

Melt butter in small pan, add onion, cook, stirring, until soft. Add brandy and peppercorns, cook, stirring, 2 minutes. Add cream and milk, stir until heated through.

Serves 4. Makes about ¾ cup (180ml).

■ Recipe can be made 2 hours ahead.
■ Storage: Covered, in refrigerator.
■ Freeze: Not suitable.
■ Microwave: Suitable.
Also suitable for: Fish, beef, pork.

SOUR CREAM SAUCE

90g butter
2 medium (300g) onions, chopped
2 tablespoons plain flour
3 teaspoons brown sugar
1 teaspoon dry mustard
1½ cups (375ml) milk
1 cup (250ml) sour cream
2 tablespoons chopped fresh parsley

Heat butter in pan, add onions, cook, stirring, until soft. Stir in flour, sugar and mustard, stir over heat until mixture is dry and grainy. Gradually stir in milk and cream, stir over heat until sauce boils and thickens; add parsley.

Serves 8. Makes about 3 cups (750ml).

■ Sauce can be made a day ahead.
■ Storage: Covered, in refrigerator.
■ Freeze: Not suitable.
■ Microwave: Suitable.
Also suitable for: Fish, chicken.

SAUCES for desserts

You can quickly dress up cakes, ice-cream, waffles, pastry, fruit and more with one of our luscious sauces.

ROCKY ROAD SAUCE

200g dark chocolate, finely chopped
1 cup (250ml) cream
¾ cup (90g) chopped, packaged
**   white marshmallows**
¼ cup (50g) red glace cherries
¼ cup (35g) crushed mixed nuts

Combine chocolate and cream in heatproof bowl over pan of simmering water, stir until chocolate is melted and mixture is smooth. Cool to room temperature; stir in remaining ingredients.

Serves 6. Makes about 2 cups (500ml).

■ Sauce can be made a day ahead.
■ Storage: Covered, in refrigerator.
■ Freeze: Not suitable.
■ Microwave: Suitable.

Suitable for: Ice-cream.

RIGHT: From left: Mocha Sauce, Rocky Road Sauce.

Plates from Royal Doulton.

MOCHA SAUCE

½ cup (45g) roasted coffee beans
⅓ cup (75g) caster sugar
40g butter
2 tablespoons dark rum
300ml cream
90g dark chocolate, finely chopped

Blend or process beans until coarsely chopped. Combine beans, sugar and butter in pan, stir over heat, without boiling, until sugar is dissolved. Add rum, cook, stirring, 1 minute, add cream, simmer 3 minutes. Strain sauce, discard beans. Add chocolate, stir until chocolate is melted and sauce is smooth and thick. Serve hot or cold.

Serves 4. Makes about 1¼ cups (310ml).

■ Sauce can be made a day ahead.
■ Storage: Covered, in refrigerator.
■ Freeze: Not suitable.
■ Microwave: Suitable.

Suitable for: Ice-cream, cakes, mousses, poached pears.

HOT ORANGE SABAYON SAUCE

2 tablespoons caster sugar
3 egg yolks
2 tablespoons water
1 tablespoon Grand Marnier
2 tablespoons cream

Combine sugar, egg yolks, water and liqueur in heatproof bowl, whisk over pan of simmering water until light and frothy, remove from heat. Stir in cream; serve sauce immediately.

Serves 6. Makes about 2 cups (500ml).

- Recipe must be made close to serving.
- Freeze: Not suitable.
- Microwave: Not suitable.

Suitable for: Steamed pudding, fresh fruit, cakes.

HONEY YOGURT CREAM

300ml thickened cream
¼ cup (60ml) honey
1 cup (250ml) plain yogurt

Beat cream in small bowl with electric mixer until soft peaks form, add honey, beat until combined. Gently fold yogurt into cream mixture.

Makes about 3 cups (750ml).

- Recipe can be made a day ahead.
- Storage: Covered, in refrigerator.
- Freeze: Not suitable.

PASSIONFRUIT CUSTARD

2 tablespoons caster sugar
2 egg yolks
½ cup (125ml) milk
⅔ cup (160ml) cream
1 teaspoon cornflour
1 teaspoon custard powder
¼ cup (60ml) milk, extra
2 tablespoons passionfruit pulp

Beat sugar and egg yolks in small bowl with electric mixer until thick and creamy. Combine milk and cream in pan, bring to boil, remove from heat. Beat hot milk mixture gradually into egg yolk mixture, return to pan. Stir in blended cornflour, custard powder and extra milk, stir over heat until mixture boils and thickens. Stir in passionfruit; cool, cover, refrigerate.

Serves 6. Makes about 1¾ cups (430ml)

- Recipe can be made a day ahead.
- Storage: Covered, in refrigerator.
- Freeze: Not suitable.
- Microwave: Not suitable.

Suitable for: Meringues, fresh fruit, steamed pudding.

RICH CARAMEL SAUCE

90g butter
¾ cup (150g) firmly packed brown sugar
300ml cream
3 teaspoons cornflour
1 tablespoon water
¼ cup (30g) chopped hazelnuts

Melt butter in pan, add sugar, stir over heat, without boiling, until sugar is dissolved. Stir in cream and blended cornflour and water, stir over heat until mixture boils and thickens. Stir in nuts.

Serves 6. Makes about 2 cups (500ml).

- Recipe can be made 2 days ahead.
- Storage: Covered, in refrigerator.
- Microwave: Suitable.
- Freeze: Not suitable.

CHOCOLATE FUDGE SAUCE

½ cup (125ml) cream
¼ cup (55g) caster sugar
125g dark chocolate, chopped
1 tablespoon brandy

Combine cream and sugar in pan, stir over heat, without boiling, until sugar is dissolved. Bring to boil, remove from heat, add chocolate and brandy, stir until chocolate is melted and sauce is smooth. Serve hot or warm.

Serves 4. Makes about 1 cup (250ml).

- Recipe best made just before serving.
- Freeze: Not suitable.
- Microwave: Suitable.

Suitable for: Ice-cream, waffles, fresh fruit, cakes.

LEFT: From back: Honey Yogurt Cream, Hot Orange Sabayon Sauce, Passionfruit Custard.

China and glassware from Villeroy & Boch.

ABOVE: From left: Rich Caramel Sauce, Chocolate Fudge Sauce.

Plates and bowls from Barbara's Storehouse.

KIWI FRUIT AND MINT SAUCE

**9 medium (800g) kiwi fruit,
   peeled, chopped**
¼ cup (55g) caster sugar
1 tablespoon chopped fresh mint
1½ tablespoons gin

Blend or process kiwi fruit until smooth; push through sieve. Stir in sugar, mint and gin, stir until sugar is dissolved. Refrigerate until cold.

Serves 6. Makes about 3 cups (750ml).

▪ Sauce can be made 2 days ahead.
▪ Storage: Covered, in refrigerator.
▪ Freeze: Not suitable.

Suitable for: Ice-cream, sorbet, fruit.

STRAWBERRY RHUBARB SAUCE

2 cups (230g) chopped rhubarb
250g strawberries, halved
½ cup (110g) caster sugar
2 tablespoons water
1 tablespoon Grand Marnier
1 tablespoon chopped fresh mint

Combine rhubarb, strawberries, sugar and water in pan, stir over heat until sugar is dissolved. Simmer, uncovered, about 10 minutes or until rhubarb is soft and mixture is thickened. Blend or process until smooth; cool. Stir in liqueur and mint.

Serves 4. Makes about 2 cups (500ml).

▪ Sauce can be made a day ahead.
▪ Storage: Covered, in refrigerator.
▪ Freeze: Suitable.
▪ Microwave: Suitable.

*Suitable for: Ice-cream, cakes,
apples, berries.*

WARM MARSALA SAUCE

60g butter
**¾ cup (150g) firmly packed
   brown sugar**
¼ cup (60ml) marsala
¾ cup (180ml) thickened cream

Combine butter, sugar and marsala in pan, stir over low heat until butter is melted and mixture heated through. Stir in cream. Serve warm.

Serves 6. Makes about 1½ cups (375ml).

▪ Recipe can be made a day ahead.
▪ Storage: Covered, in refrigerator.
▪ Freeze: Not suitable.
▪ Microwave: Suitable.

*Suitable for: Cakes, ice-cream, fresh
fruit, crepes, choux puffs.*

APPLE BUTTERSCOTCH SAUCE

2 large (400g) apples, peeled, thinly sliced
1 tablespoon caster sugar
¼ cup (60ml) water
¼ teaspoon ground cinnamon
60g butter
⅔ cup (130g) firmly packed brown sugar
⅔ cup (160ml) thickened cream

Combine apples, caster sugar, water and cinnamon in pan, simmer, covered, about 10 minutes or until apples are tender; drain, reserve apples. Melt butter in pan, add brown sugar and cream, stir until combined. Simmer, uncovered, without stirring, 5 minutes until hot. Stir in reserved apples, cook, stirring, until apples are heated through.

Serves 4. Makes about 2½ cups (625ml).

▪ Recipe can be made 3 hours ahead.
▪ Storage: Covered, in refrigerator.
▪ Freeze: Not suitable.
▪ Microwave: Not suitable.

Suitable for: Crepes, waffles, ice-cream.

RIGHT: From left: Warm Marsala Sauce, Apple Butterscotch Sauce.
ABOVE: From left: Kiwi Fruit and Mint Sauce, Strawberry Rhubarb Sauce.

Above: Plates from Barbara's Storehouse.

RASPBERRY LEMON BUTTER SAUCE

150g frozen raspberries, thawed
3 egg yolks
¼ cup (55g) caster sugar
1 tablespoon grated lemon rind
2 tablespoons lemon juice
100g unsalted butter, chopped

Blend or process raspberries until smooth, push through fine sieve, discard seeds. Combine raspberry puree and remaining ingredients in small pan, whisk constantly over low heat, without boiling, until mixture thickens slightly. Remove pan from heat, transfer mixture to bowl immediately; cool.

Serves 4 to 6. Makes about 1¼ cups (310ml).

- Sauce can be made 2 days ahead.
- Storage: Covered, in refrigerator.
- Freeze: Not suitable.
- Microwave: Not suitable.

Suitable for: Ice-cream, meringues, sorbets, fresh fruit, cakes, choux puffs.

PEACH SAUCE

2 teaspoons cornflour
1 cup (250ml) peach nectar
2 teaspoons caster sugar
¼ teaspoon ground cinnamon
2 tablespoons peach liqueur
2 drained canned peach halves, thinly sliced

Blend cornflour with 1 tablespoon of the nectar in small pan, stir in remaining nectar, sugar and cinnamon. Stir over heat until mixture boils and thickens, cool. Stir in liqueur and peaches.

Serves 4. Makes about 1 cup (250ml).

- Recipe can be made a day ahead.
- Storage: Covered, in refrigerator.
- Freeze: Not suitable.
- Microwave: Suitable.

Suitable for: Ice-cream, meringues, fresh fruit, cakes.

LEFT: From left: Raspberry Lemon Butter Sauce, Peach Sauce.
RIGHT: From back: Creme Anglaise, Brandy Butter.

Left: China from Waterford Wedgwood.

CREME ANGLAISE

1 vanilla bean
1½ cups (375ml) milk
1 tablespoon caster sugar
4 egg yolks
¼ cup (55g) caster sugar, extra

Split vanilla bean open. Combine milk, vanilla bean and sugar in small pan, bring to boil. Remove from heat, stand, covered, 20 minutes.

Combine egg yolks and extra sugar in bowl; whisk until smooth. Slowly pour milk mixture onto egg mixture, whisking constantly. Return mixture to pan, stir constantly over low heat, without boiling, until mixture thickens slightly and coats the back of a wooden spoon. Strain mixture, cover surface, refrigerate until cold.

Serves 6. Makes about 1½ cups (375ml).

- Recipe can be made 3 days ahead.
- Storage: Cover surface with plastic wrap, store in refrigerator.
- Freeze: Not suitable.
- Microwave: Not suitable.

BRANDY BUTTER

100g soft unsalted butter
1 cup (160g) pure icing sugar
1½ tablespoons brandy

Cream butter in small bowl with electric mixer until light and fluffy, gradually add sifted icing sugar and brandy, beat until smooth. Refrigerate 1 hour or until firm.

Serves 6. Makes about 1 cup (250ml).

- Recipe can be made a week ahead.
- Storage: Covered, in refrigerator.
- Freeze: Suitable.

Suitable for: Christmas pudding.

CHOCOLATE SAUCE

125g dark chocolate, melted
¼ cup (40g) icing sugar mixture
300ml thickened cream
2 tablespoons Kahlua
1 teaspoon vanilla essence

Place chocolate in bowl, stir in sifted icing sugar, cream, liqueur and essence; stir until smooth.

Serves 4. Makes about 2 cups (500ml).

▦ Sauce can be made a day ahead.
▦ Storage: Covered, in refrigerator.
▦ Freeze: Not suitable.
▦ Microwave: Chocolate suitable.

Suitable for: Ice-cream, waffles.

BUTTERSCOTCH SAUCE

1 cup (200g) firmly packed brown sugar
1 cup (250ml) cream
150g butter, chopped

Combine all ingredients in pan, stir over heat until sugar is dissolved and butter is melted. Simmer, uncovered, 3 minutes.

Serves 4. Makes about 2 cups (500ml).

▦ Sauce can be made 3 days ahead.
▦ Storage: Covered, in refrigerator.
▦ Freeze: Suitable.
▦ Microwave: Suitable.

Suitable for: Waffles, crepes, bananas.

PEANUT CARAMEL SAUCE

125g butter
1 cup (200g) firmly packed brown sugar
400g can sweetened condensed milk
¼ cup (60ml) sour cream
½ cup (125ml) thickened cream
⅓ cup (80ml) smooth peanut butter

Melt butter in heavy-based pan, add sugar and milk, stir over heat, without boiling, until sugar is dissolved. Stir over high heat about 5 minutes or until mixture is golden brown. Remove from heat, allow bubbles to subside. Stir in creams and peanut butter. Serve warm.

Serves 8. Makes about 3 cups (750ml).

▦ Recipe can be made a week ahead.
▦ Storage: Covered, in refrigerator.
▦ Freeze: Not suitable.
▦ Microwave: Not suitable.

Suitable for: Waffles, ice-cream.

WHITE CHOCOLATE SAUCE

½ cup (125ml) milk
½ cup (125ml) cream
250g white chocolate, grated
2 teaspoons Kahlua
pinch ground nutmeg

Combine milk and cream in pan, stir over heat until hot, do not boil. Remove from heat, add chocolate, stir until chocolate is melted and sauce is smooth. Stir in liqueur and nutmeg.

Serves 4. Makes about 1½ cups (375ml).

▦ Recipe can be made a day ahead.
▦ Storage: Covered, in refrigerator.
▦ Freeze: Not suitable.
▦ Microwave: Suitable.

Suitable for: Cakes, fresh fruit.

ABOVE: From left: Chocolate Cherry Sauce, Chocolate Hazelnut Sauce.
LEFT: Clockwise from top left: Butterscotch Sauce, White Chocolate Sauce, Peanut Caramel Sauce, Chocolate Sauce.

Left: Bowls from Villeroy & Boch. Above: Plates from Royal Doulton.

CHOCOLATE CHERRY SAUCE

180g dark chocolate, finely chopped
300ml cream
¼ cup (60ml) cherry brandy liqueur

Heat chocolate and cream in heatproof bowl over pan of simmering water, stir until chocolate is melted, add cherry brandy; stir until smooth. Serve hot or cold.

Serves 4. Makes about 1¾ cups (430ml).

▓ Sauce can be made a day ahead.
▓ Storage: Covered, in refrigerator.
▓ Freeze: Suitable.
▓ Microwave: Suitable.

Suitable for: Ice-cream, profiteroles.

CHOCOLATE HAZELNUT SAUCE

1 cup (250ml) cream
½ cup (125ml) chocolate hazelnut spread
2 tablespoons Tia Maria

Combine cream and spread in pan, stir over heat until smooth, stir in liqueur. Refrigerate sauce until thickened.

Serves 4 to 6. Makes about 1¾ cups (430ml).

▓ Sauce can be made 2 days ahead.
▓ Storage: Covered, in refrigerator.
▓ Freeze: Not suitable
▓ Microwave: Suitable.

Suitable for: Ice-cream, pears, bananas, waffles, cakes.

ORANGE AND LIME GLAZE

1 medium (170g) orange
1 medium (80g) lime
1 cup (250ml) orange juice
¼ cup (60ml) lime juice
⅓ cup (80ml) honey
1 tablespoon caster sugar
2½ teaspoons cornflour
3 teaspoons water
2 tablespoons Grand Marnier

Using a vegetable peeler, peel rinds thinly from orange and lime, avoiding any white pith; slice rind into thin strips. Place rind in pan, cover with cold water, bring to boil; drain. Repeat boiling and draining twice. Combine rind, juices, honey and sugar in pan, simmer 2 minutes, stir in blended cornflour and water, stir over heat until mixture boils and thickens. Stir in liqueur. Serve warm.

Makes about 1⅔ cups (410ml).

▦ Sauce can be made a day ahead.
▦ Storage: Covered, in refrigerator.
▦ Freeze: Suitable.
▦ Microwave: Suitable.

Suitable for: Crepes, ice-cream.

PRALINE SAUCE

½ cup (70g) slivered almonds, toasted
1 cup (220g) caster sugar
½ cup (125ml) water
300ml cream

Place almonds onto oven tray covered with baking paper. Combine sugar and water in pan, stir over heat, without boiling, until sugar is dissolved, boil, uncovered, without stirring, until golden brown, pour over almonds; stand until set. Break praline into small pieces, process until fine. Combine praline and cream; mix well.

Serves 6. Makes about 2 cups (500ml).

▦ Praline can be made 3 days ahead.
▦ Storage: Praline in airtight container.
▦ Freeze: Not suitable.
▦ Microwave: Not suitable.

Suitable for: Waffles, ice-cream, pancakes, steamed pudding.

TANGY LEMON SAUCE

1 cup (220g) caster sugar
1½ tablespoons arrowroot
2 cups (500ml) milk
3 egg yolks
1 teaspoon grated lemon rind
⅓ cup (80ml) lemon juice

Combine sugar and arrowroot in pan, gradually stir in milk, stir over heat until mixture boils and thickens; remove from heat, cool slightly. Quickly whisk in egg yolks, then rind and juice.

Serves 8. Makes about 2½ cups (625ml).

▦ Recipe can be made a day ahead.
▦ Storage: Covered, in refrigerator.
▦ Freeze: Not suitable.
▦ Microwave: Suitable.

BELOW: Clockwise from left: Orange and Lime Glaze, Tangy Lemon Sauce, Praline Sauce.
BELOW RIGHT: Grapefruit Glaze.
RIGHT: From left: Lemon Sauce, Pistachio Sauce.

Below: Plates from Waterford Wedgwood.
Below right: Plate from Royal Doulton.
Right: China from Villeroy & Boch.

LEMON SAUCE

2 tablespoons caster sugar
1 tablespoon grated lemon rind
½ cup (125ml) lemon juice
2 egg yolks
¼ cup (55g) caster sugar, extra
2 tablespoons cream

Combine sugar, rind and juice in pan, stir over heat, without boiling, until sugar is dissolved; bring to boil, cool 5 minutes, strain. Place lemon mixture into small heatproof bowl, whisk in egg yolks and extra sugar, whisk over pan of simmering water until sauce is thickened slightly; cool. Strain mixture, whisk in cream.

Serves 4. Makes about ⅔ cup (160ml).

- Recipe can be made a day ahead.
- Storage: Covered, in refrigerator.
- Freeze: Not suitable.
- Microwave: Not suitable.

Suitable for: Cakes, meringues, pastries.

GRAPEFRUIT GLAZE

1 cup (250ml) fresh grapefruit juice
¼ cup (60ml) lime juice
¼ cup (60ml) orange juice
¼ cup (60ml) honey
1 tablespoon dark rum
3 teaspoons cornflour
3 teaspoons water

Combine strained juices, honey and rum in pan, stir in blended cornflour and water, stir over heat until mixture boils and thickens slightly.

Serves 4. Makes about 1¼ cups (310ml).

- Recipe best made just before serving.
- Freeze: Not suitable.
- Microwave: Suitable.

PISTACHIO SAUCE

¼ cup (35g) shelled pistachio
**   nuts, toasted**
2 tablespoons blanched
**   almonds, toasted**
¼ cup (55g) caster sugar
1 cup (250ml) milk
2 egg yolks

Rub pistachio nuts in a clean tea towel to remove as much skin as possible. Blend or process pistachios and almonds with half the sugar until finely crushed. Combine nut mixture and milk in pan, bring to boil, remove from heat, cover, stand 30 minutes. Strain milk into clean pan; discard nuts. Whisk egg yolks and remaining sugar until combined. Reheat milk to just below boil, whisk milk into yolk mixture; return mixture to pan, stir over low heat without boiling until sauce thickens slightly. Remove from heat, whisk further minute.

Serves 4. Makes about ¾ cup (180ml).

- Sauce can be made 2 days ahead.
- Storage: Covered, in refrigerator.
- Freeze: Not suitable.
- Microwave: Not suitable.

Suitable for: Ice-cream, waffles.

BRANDY CREAM SAUCE

1 cup (250ml) cream
½ cup (125ml) milk
1 tablespoon caster sugar
4 egg yolks
¼ cup (55g) caster sugar, extra
2 tablespoons brandy

Combine cream, milk and sugar in small pan, bring to boil; remove from heat. Beat egg yolks and extra sugar in small bowl with electric mixer until thick, gradually pour milk mixture into egg mixture, beating constantly. Return mixture to pan, stir over low heat, without boiling, until mixture is slightly thickened and coats the back of a wooden spoon. Strain mixture, stir in brandy. Serve sauce warm or cold.

Serves 6. Makes about 1½ cups (375ml).

- Sauce can be made 3 days ahead.
- Storage: Covered, in refrigerator.
- Freeze: Not suitable.
- Microwave: Not suitable.

Suitable for: Christmas pudding, steamed pudding, apple pie.

COFFEE CUSTARD

6 egg yolks
⅔ cup (150g) caster sugar
1 cup (250ml) milk
1 cup (250ml) cream
⅓ cup (30g) roasted coffee beans

Whisk egg yolks and sugar together in bowl until combined. Combine milk, cream and beans in pan, stir over low heat until mixture comes to boil; remove from heat; strain. Gradually whisk hot milk mixture into egg yolk mixture. Return mixture to pan, stir over low heat, without boiling, about 10 minutes or until mixture is slightly thickened and coats the back of a wooden spoon.

Serves 6. Makes about 2 cups (500ml).

- Sauce can be made day ahead.
- Storage: Covered, in refrigerator.
- Freeze: Not suitable.
- Microwave: Not suitable.

Suitable for: Ice-cream, cakes, crepes.

LEFT: From left: Coffee Custard, Brandy Cream Sauce.
ABOVE: Passionfruit Sauce.
RIGHT: From back: Brandied Apricot Sauce, Strawberry Sauce.

Above: Plate from Royal Doulton. Right: China from Waterford Wedgwood.

BRANDIED APRICOT SAUCE

½ cup (about 75g) chopped dried apricots
1¼ cups (310ml) water
2 tablespoons caster sugar
¼ teaspoon ground cinnamon
2 teaspoons brandy

Combine apricots, water, sugar and cinnamon in pan, simmer, covered, about 5 minutes or until apricots are soft, cool. Blend or process apricot mixture with brandy until smooth.

Serves 4. Makes about 1¼ cups (310ml).

- ■ Recipe can be made a day ahead.
- ■ Storage: Covered, in refrigerator.
- ■ Freeze: Not suitable.
- ■ Microwave: Suitable.

Suitable for: Pancakes, ice-cream, cakes.

STRAWBERRY SAUCE

500g strawberries
¼ cup (40g) icing sugar mixture
2 teaspoons Grand Marnier

Blend or process all ingredients until smooth; strain.

Serves 4 to 6. Makes about 1¾ cups (430ml).

- ■ Recipe can be made 2 days ahead.
- ■ Storage: Covered, in refrigerator.
- ■ Freeze: Not suitable.

Suitable for: Tarts, sponges, fresh fruit, ice-cream.

PASSIONFRUIT SAUCE

⅔ (160ml) cup passionfruit pulp (about 8 passionfruit)
¼ cup (55g) caster sugar
½ cup (125ml) water
2 teaspoons cornflour
1 tablespoon water, extra

Combine unstrained passionfruit pulp, sugar and water in small pan, stir over heat until sugar is dissolved. Stir in blended cornflour and extra water, stir over heat until mixture boils and thickens slightly. Strain sauce, return 3 teaspoons of seeds to sauce, discard remaining seeds. Serve cold.

Serves 4. Makes about ½ cup (125ml).

- ■ Recipe can be made a day ahead.
- ■ Storage: Covered, in refrigerator.
- ■ Freeze: Suitable.
- ■ Microwave: Suitable.

Suitable for: Ice-cream, cakes, mousses, fresh fruit.

CITRUS SAUCE FLAMBE

Do not ignite sauce while exhuast fan is operating. Use a long taper to ignite hot sauce.

125g butter
½ cup (110g) caster sugar
1½ cups (375ml) orange juice
2 tablespoons lemon juice
½ cup (125ml) Grand Marnier

Melt butter in pan, add sugar. Cook over low heat until sugar is dissolved and begins to caramelise. Add juices, stir over high heat until caramelised sugar is dissolved. Remove from heat, add liqueur, set aflame immediately. When flames subside, return sauce to heat, boil until reduced to 1½ cups (375ml).

Serves 4. Makes 1½ cups (375ml)

- Recipe best made just before serving.
- Freeze: Not suitable.
- Microwave: Not suitable.

Suitable for: Crepes, fresh fruit, ice-cream.

GINGER SAUCE

¾ cup (180ml) water
½ cup (125ml) golden syrup
¼ cup (100g) chopped glace ginger
2 teaspoons cornflour
2 teaspoons water, extra
30g butter

Blend or process water, syrup and ginger until smooth. Transfer ginger mixture to pan, stir in blended cornflour and extra water; stir over heat until mixture boils and thickens slightly. Remove from heat, whisk in butter until melted. Serve sauce warm or cold.

Serves 4. Makes about 1½ cups (375ml).

- Sauce can be made a day ahead.
- Storage: Covered, in refrigerator.
- Freeze: Not suitable.
- Microwave: Suitable.

Suitable for: Waffles, crepes, bananas, ice-cream, souffles, cakes.

TROPICAL FRUIT SAUCE

125g butter
½ cup (110g) caster sugar
1 teaspoon grated lime rind
1 teaspoon grated orange rind
1¼ cups (310ml) tropical fruit juice
2 tablespoons lime juice
2 medium (340g) oranges, segmented
2 medium passionfruit
2 medium bananas, sliced
2 tablespoons Malibu

Melt butter in pan, add sugar, stir over heat, without boiling, until sugar is dissolved. Stir in rinds and juices, boil, uncovered, stirring occasionally until sauce is golden brown. Stir in oranges, passionfruit and bananas, stir over low heat until bananas are just soft. Stir in Malibu.

Serves 6. Makes about 3 cups (750ml).

- Recipe best made just before serving.
- Freeze: Not suitable.
- Microwave: Not suitable.

Suitable for: Any dessert not containing fruit.

BLUEBERRY BUTTER SAUCE

¼ cup (55g) caster sugar
¾ cup (180ml) water
3 teaspoons cornflour
1 tablespoon lemon juice
1 cup (150g) fresh or
    frozen blueberries
30g butter
½ teaspoon ground cinnamon

Combine sugar and water in pan, stir in blended cornflour and juice, stir over heat until mixture boils and thickens. Add blueberries, simmer 2 minutes. Add butter and cinnamon, stir over heat until butter is melted. Blend or process until smooth, strain sauce. Serve hot or cold.

Serves 6. Makes about 1¼ cups (310ml).

■ Sauce can be made 3 days ahead.
■ Storage: Covered, in refrigerator.
■ Freeze: Not suitable.
■ Microwave: Suitable.

Suitable for: Fresh fruit, ice-cream, mousses.

MELBA SAUCE

425g can sliced peaches in syrup
400g fresh raspberries
½ cup (110g) caster sugar
2 teaspoons cornflour
2 tablespoons peach liqueur

Drain peaches; reserve ⅔ cup (160ml) syrup. Blend or process peaches and berries until smooth; strain, discard seeds. Pour peach mixture into pan, add sugar, stir over heat, without boiling, until sugar is dissolved. Stir in blended cornflour and reserved syrup, stir over heat until mixture boils and thickens. Stir in liqueur. Serve warm or cold.

Serves 6. Makes about 3 cups (750ml).

■ Sauce can be made a day ahead.
■ Storage: Covered, in refrigerator.
■ Freeze: Suitable.
■ Microwave: Suitable.

Suitable for: Fresh fruit, ice-cream, crepes, waffles.

MANGO AND LIME SAUCE

2 medium (860g) mangoes, chopped
2½ tablespoons lime juice
1 tablespoon Amaretto

Blend or process mangoes, juice and liqueur until smooth.

Serves 6. Makes about 1½ cups (375ml).

■ Sauce can be made a day ahead.
■ Storage: Covered, in refrigerator.
■ Freeze: Suitable.

Suitable for: Fresh fruit, ice-cream, mousses, cakes, pastries.

ABOVE: From left: Citrus Sauce Flambe, Ginger Sauce.
RIGHT: Clockwise from left: Tropical Fruit Sauce, Blueberry Butter Sauce, Melba Sauce, Mango and Lime Sauce.

Above: Plates from Villeroy & Boch.
Right: Glassware from Zuhause.

SAUCES
basic recipes

These classics form the framework on which most sauces are based. They complement a variety of dishes. Experiment with seasonings to taste.

BASIC RED WINE SAUCE

30g butter
60g French shallots, finely chopped
1 clove garlic, crushed
1½ tablespoons plain flour
2 teaspoons chopped fresh thyme
⅓ cup (80ml) dry red wine
1 cup (250ml) beef stock

Melt butter in pan, add shallots and garlic, cook, stirring, until shallots are soft. Stir in flour, stir over heat until lightly browned. Remove from heat, gradually stir in combined thyme, wine and stock, stir over heat until sauce boils and thickens; strain.

Serves 4. Makes about 1 cup (250ml).

■ Sauce can be made a day ahead.
■ Storage: Covered, in refrigerator.
■ Freeze: Suitable.
■ Microwave: Suitable.

BASIC TOMATO SAUCE

2 tablespoons olive oil
1 medium (150g) onion,
   finely chopped
3 cloves garlic, crushed
¼ cup (60ml) dry red wine
2 x 410g cans tomatoes
2 tablespoons tomato paste
1 teaspoon sugar
1 tablespoon chopped fresh thyme
1 tablespoon chopped fresh basil

Heat oil in pan, add onion and garlic, cook, stirring, until onion is soft. Add wine, simmer, uncovered, until reduced by half. Stir in undrained crushed tomatoes, paste, sugar and thyme, simmer, uncovered, about 10 minutes or until thick; add basil.

Serves 6. Makes about 3 cups (750ml).

■ Recipe can be made 2 days ahead.
■ Storage: Covered, in refrigerator.
■ Freeze: Suitable.
■ Microwave: Not suitable.

BASIC BARBECUE SAUCE

2 tablespoons olive oil
2 medium (300g) onions, sliced
2 cloves garlic, crushed
¼ cup (60ml) red wine vinegar
¼ cup (50g) firmly packed
   brown sugar
2 tablespoons Dijon mustard
2 tablespoons Worcestershire sauce
410g can tomatoes
¼ cup (60ml) tomato paste

Heat oil in pan, add onions and garlic, cook, stirring, until onions are soft. Stir in remaining ingredients, simmer, uncovered, about 15 minutes or until thick. Blend or process sauce until smooth; push through sieve. Serve warm or cold.

Serves 8. Makes about 1½ cups (375ml).

■ Sauce can be made 2 days ahead.
■ Storage: Covered, in refrigerator.
■ Freeze: Suitable.
■ Microwave: Not suitable.

RIGHT: Clockwise from front: Basic Barbecue Sauce, Basic Red Wine Sauce, Basic Tomato Sauce,

Cast iron saucepan from Accoutrement; sauce boat from Home and Garden on The Mall.

ANCHOVY BUTTER

125g soft butter
56g can anchovy fillets, drained,
finely chopped
2 tablespoons chopped fresh basil
1 clove garlic, crushed

Combine all ingredients in bowl; mix well.
Serves 6.

- Recipe can be made 3 days ahead.
- Storage: Covered, in refrigerator.
- Freeze: Suitable.

MUSTARD BUTTER

125g soft butter
2 tablespoons seeded mustard
2 tablespoons chopped fresh chives
1 teaspoon grated lemon rind

Combine all ingredients in bowl; mix well.
Serves 6.

- Recipe can be made 3 days ahead.
- Storage: Covered, in refrigerator.
- Freeze: Suitable.

CORIANDER CURRY BUTTER

1 teaspoon mild curry powder
1 teaspoon ground cumin
1 clove garlic, crushed
125g soft butter
1 tablespoon chopped fresh
coriander

Combine curry powder, cumin and garlic
in pan, stir over heat until fragrant; cool.
Combine spice mixture, butter and
coriander in bowl; mix well.

Serves 6.

- Recipe can be made 3 days ahead.
- Storage: Covered, in refrigerator.
- Freeze: Suitable.

TOMATO OLIVE BUTTER

125g soft butter
2 tablespoons tomato paste
1½ tablespoons chopped seeded
black olives
1 clove garlic, crushed
¼ cup (20g) grated fresh
parmesan cheese

Combine all ingredients in bowl, mix well.
Serves 6.

- Recipe can be made 3 days ahead.
- Storage: Covered in refrigerator.
- Freeze: Suitable.

BASIC CHEESE SAUCE

50g butter
¼ cup (35g) plain flour
1½ cups (375ml) milk
⅓ cup (40g) grated tasty
cheddar cheese

Melt butter in pan, stir in flour, stir over
heat until mixture is dry and grainy.
Remove from heat, gradually stir in milk,
stir over heat until sauce boils and thickens, cool slightly; stir in cheese.

Serves 4. Makes about 1¼ cups (310ml).

- Sauce best made just before serving.
- Freeze: Not suitable.
- Microwave: Suitable.

BECHAMEL SAUCE

1 cup (250ml) milk
1 bay leaf
1 slice onion
1 sprig fresh parsley
1 sprig fresh thyme
4 black peppercorns
20g butter
1 tablespoon plain flour

Combine milk, bay leaf, onion, parsley,
thyme and peppercorns in pan, bring to
boil, strain; cool. Melt butter in pan, stir in
flour, stir over heat until dry and grainy.
Remove from heat, gradually stir in milk,
stir over heat until sauce boils and thickens.

Serves 4. Makes about ¾ cup (180ml).

- Sauce best made just before serving.
- Freeze: Not suitable.
- Microwave: Suitable.

VELOUTE SAUCE

50g butter
¼ cup (35g) plain flour
2 cups (500ml) chicken stock
1 bay leaf
1 sprig thyme
1 sprig parsley
5 black peppercorns

Melt butter in pan, stir in flour, stir over
heat until bubbling. Remove from heat,
gradually stir in stock, bay leaf, thyme,
parsley and peppercorns. Simmer gently,
uncovered, 30 minutes, stirring occasionally. Skim surface of sauce during
cooking. Strain sauce through fine sieve.

Serves 4. Makes about 1¼ cups (310ml).

- Sauce best made just before serving.
- Freeze: Not suitable.
- Microwave: Not suitable.

*BELOW: Clockwise from left: Veloute Sauce,
Basic Cheese Sauce, Bechamel Sauce.*

*LEFT: Clockwise from back left: Tomato Olive
Butter, Anchovy Butter, Mustard Butter,
Coriander Curry Butter.*

HOLLANDAISE

1 tablespoon water
¼ cup (60ml) white wine vinegar
2 teaspoons lemon juice
1 bay leaf
2 green shallots, finely chopped
1 teaspoon black peppercorns
3 egg yolks
185g butter, melted

Simmer water, vinegar, juice, bay leaf, shallots and peppercorns in pan until liquid is reduced to 2 tablespoons; strain and reserve liquid; cool. Combine egg yolks and vinegar mixture in heatproof bowl over pan of simmering water; do not allow water to touch base of bowl. Whisk mixture constantly until thickened. Add butter gradually in a thin stream, whisking constantly until mixture has thickened. If mixture is too thick, stir in 1 to 2 tablespoons of hot water to give a pouring consistency.

Recipe makes about 1⅓ cups (330ml).

■ Recipe best made just before serving.
■ Freeze: Not suitable.
■ Microwave: Not suitable.

BEARNAISE

½ cup (125ml) white vinegar
3 green shallots, finely chopped
8 black peppercorns
1 bay leaf
1 teaspoon fresh tarragon leaves
4 egg yolks
250g butter, melted, cooled

Simmer vinegar, shallots, peppercorns, bay leaf and tarragon in pan until liquid is reduced to 2 tablespoons; strain and reserve liquid. Place egg yolks in heatproof bowl over pan of simmering water; do not allow water to touch base of bowl. Whisk in reserved liquid. Place pan over low heat so water is barely simmering. Add butter gradually in a thin stream. Whisk constantly until mixture has thickened. If mixture is too thick stir in 1 to 2 tablespoons hot water.

Recipe makes about 1¼ cups (310ml).

■ Recipe best made just before serving.
■ Freeze: Not suitable.
■ Microwave: Not suitable.

BEURRE BLANC

2 green shallots, finely chopped
2 tablespoons fish stock
2 tablespoons white wine vinegar
¼ cup (60ml) dry white wine
250g cold butter, chopped

Boil shallots, stock, vinegar and wine in small pan until reduced to 2 tablespoons; strain and reserve liquid. Return liquid to pan. Whisk in 2 cubes of butter. Whisk in remaining butter over low heat, 1 cube at a time, until the sauce has thickened. The sauce will thicken to the consistency of pouring cream.

Recipe makes about 1¼ cups (310ml).

■ Recipe best made just before serving.
■ Freeze: Not suitable.
■ Microwave: Not suitable.

ABOVE: Clockwise from back: Beurre Blanc, Bearnaise, Hollandaise.

China from Accoutrement; saucepan from Whitehill Silver and Plate Co Pty Ltd.

BASIC MAYONNAISE

2 egg yolks
1 tablespoon lemon juice
1 teaspoon Dijon mustard
½ cup (125ml) olive oil
½ cup (125ml) light olive oil
2 tablespoons hot water,
   approximately

Blend or process egg yolks, juice and mustard until smooth. Add combined oils gradually in a thin stream while motor is operating; add enough water to bring mayonnaise to desired consistency. Blend until smooth.

Makes about 1 cup (250ml).

■ Recipe can be made a week ahead.
■ Storage: Covered, in refrigerator.
■ Freeze: Not suitable.

BELOW: Clockwise from left: Basic Mayonnaise, Red Pepper Mayonnaise, Tartare Sauce, Herb Mayonnaise.

Glass bowls, lemon squeezer and steel basket from Home and Garden on The Mall.

TARTARE SAUCE

1 quantity basic mayonnaise
1 tablespoon chopped drained capers
1 tablespoon finely chopped gherkin
3 teaspoons finely chopped red
   Spanish onion
1 tablespoon chopped fresh parsley

Combine all ingredients in bowl; mix well.

Makes about 1¼ cups (310ml).

■ Recipe can be made 2 days ahead.
■ Storage: Covered, in refrigerator.
■ Freeze: Not suitable.

RED PEPPER MAYONNAISE

1 medium (200g) red pepper
2 egg yolks
1 tablespoon lemon juice
1 teaspoon Dijon mustard
½ cup (125ml) light olive oil
½ cup (125ml) olive oil

Quarter pepper, remove seeds and membrane. Grill pepper, skin side up, until skin blisters and blackens. Peel away skin, chop pepper. Blend pepper, egg yolks, juice and mustard until smooth. Add combined oils gradually in a thin stream while motor is operating; blend until thick.

Makes about 1½ cups (375ml).

■ Recipe can be made 2 days ahead.
■ Storage: Covered, in refrigerator.
■ Freeze: Not suitable.

HERB MAYONNAISE

2 egg yolks
1 teaspoon Dijon mustard
1 tablespoon lemon juice
1 tablespoon chopped fresh basil
1 tablespoon chopped fresh parsley
2 teaspoons chopped fresh dill
2 teaspoons chopped fresh chives
1 tablespoon chopped fresh chervil
½ cup (125ml) light olive oil
½ cup (125ml) olive oil
2 tablespoons hot water,
   approximately

Blend egg yolks, mustard, juice and herbs until smooth. Add combined oils gradually in a thin stream while motor is operating; add enough water to bring mayonnaise to desired consistency. Blend until smooth.

Makes about 1¼ cups (310ml).

■ Recipe can be made 2 days ahead.
■ Storage: Covered, in refrigerator.
■ Freeze: Not suitable .

Glossary

Names, terms and alternatives to help everyone use and understand our recipes.

AMARETTO: an almond liqueur.

ARROWROOT: used mostly for thickening.

BACON RASHERS: bacon slices.

BACCALA: salted, dried fillets of cod.

BAMBOO SHOOTS: the young tender shoots of bamboo plants, available in cans.

BEETROOT: regular round beet.

BLACK BEAN SAUCE: fermented soy beans, water and wheat flour.

BLACK BEANS, SALTED PACKAGED: fermented, salted soy beans. Canned or dried black beans can be substituted. Mash beans when cooking to release flavour.

BUTTER: use salted or unsalted (also called sweet) butter; 125g is equal to 1 stick butter.

CALVADOS: apple-flavoured brandy.

CANDLENUT: a hard nut, used to thicken curries in Malaysia and Indonesia. Available from many Asian food stores. Substitute almonds, Brazil nuts or macadamias.

CASSIS: blackcurrant-flavoured liqueur.

CHICKPEAS: garbanzos.

CHILLIES: use rubber gloves when chopping fresh chillies; they can burn your skin.

Dried crushed: available at Asian food stores.

Powder: can be substituted for fresh chillies in the proportion of 1/2 teaspoon ground chilli powder to 1 medium chopped fresh chilli.

CHOCOLATE, DARK: eating chocolate.

CHOCOLATE HAZELNUT SPREAD: Nutella.

CORIANDER: also known as cilantro and Chinese parsley; its seeds are the main ingredient of curry powder.

CORNFLOUR: cornstarch.

CREAM: fresh pouring cream; has a minimum fat content of 35 per cent.

Sour: a thick, commercially cultured soured cream.

Thickened: has a minimum fat content of 35 per cent, with the addition of a thickener, such as gelatine.

CUMQUATS: orange-coloured citrus fruit about the size of a walnut.

CUSTARD POWDER: vanilla pudding mix.

DILL PICKLES: pickled cucumbers.

ENGLISH SPINACH: young silverbeet can be substituted for English spinach.

ESSENCE: extract.

FISH SAUCE: made from the liquid drained from salted, fermented anchovies. Has a strong smell and taste; use sparingly.

FIVE-SPICE POWDER: a pungent mixture of ground spices which include cinnamon, cloves, fennel, star anise and Szechwan peppers.

FLOUR:

Plain: all-purpose flour.

FRENCH SHALLOT: very small member of the onion family with brown skin. It grows in clusters and has a definite onion/garlic flavour.

GALANGAL: is the dried root of a plant of the ginger family. It is used as a flavouring, and removed before serving or left uneaten.

GARAM MASALA: often used in Indian cooking, this spice combines cardamom, cinnamon, cloves, coriander, cumin and nutmeg in varying proportions. Sometimes pepper is included to make a hot variation.

GARLIC: can be used crushed, sliced or as whole cloves; a bulb, also known as a "knob", consists of many cloves of garlic.

GHERKIN: cornichon.

GINGER:

Fresh, green or root ginger: scrape away outside skin and grate, chop or slice.

Glace: fresh ginger root preserved in sugar syrup.

GLUCOSE SYRUP (liquid glucose): is pure sugar extracted from wheat starch combined with water to form a syrup. Used mainly in confectionery. Corn syrup can be substituted.

GOLDEN SYRUP: maple syrup, pancake syrup or honey can be substituted.

GRAND MARNIER: orange-flavoured liqueur.

GREEN BEANS: French beans.

GREEN GINGER WINE: a sweet wine infused with finely ground ginger.

GREEN PEPPERCORNS: available in cans or jars, pickled in brine.

GREEN SHALLOTS: also known as scallions and green onions.

GROUND ALMONDS: we used packaged commercially ground nuts.

HOI SIN SAUCE: is a thick sweet Chinese barbecue sauce made from salted black beans, onion and garlic.

HORSERADISH CREAM: paste of horseradish, oil, mustard and flavourings.

HORSERADISH, PREPARED: grated horseradish with flavourings.

ICING SUGAR: also known as confectioners' sugar or powdered sugar. We use icing sugar mixture, not pure icing sugar, unless specified.

JALAPENO PEPPERS: hot chillies, available in brine in bottles and cans.

JAM: conserve.

KAHLUA: a coffee-flavoured liqueur.

KIWI FRUIT: Chinese gooseberry.

KUMARA: orange-coloured sweet potato.

LAMB NOISETTES: boneless loin chop with "tail" wrapped around the meaty centre.

LEEK: a member of the onion family, it resembles the green shallot but is larger.

LEMON GRASS: available from Asian food stores. It needs to be bruised/crushed or finely chopped before using.

LENTILS: dried pulses. There are many varieties, named after their colour.

LYCHEES: peel away rough skin, remove seed before using. Also available in cans.

MACADAMIAS: Queensland or Hawaiian nuts.

MADEIRA: wine fortified with brandy.

MALIBU: a coconut-flavoured rum.

MAPLE-FLAVOURED SYRUP: golden/ pancake syrup or honey can be substituted.

MIRIN: Japanese sweet rice wine.

MARSALA: a sweet, fortified wine.

MILK: full-cream homogenised milk.

MIXED SPICE: a blend of spices consisting of cinnamon, allspice and nutmeg.

MUSHROOMS:

Button: small, unopened mushrooms with a delicate flavour.

Dried Chinese: unique in flavour.

MUSSELS: must be tightly closed when bought, indicating they are alive. Before cooking, scrub the shells with a strong brush and remove the "beards". Discard any shells that do not open after cooking.

MUSTARD:

Dijon: a sharp French mustard.

French: plain mild mustard.

Seeded: a French-style mustard with crushed mustard seeds.

NUT OF VEAL: a lean cut of meat from the leg.

OIL: polyunsaturated vegetable oil.

Extra light and light olive oil: have gone through an extra filtration process to lighten the colour and aroma. They are not lower in kilojoules.

Extra virgin olive oil: is the purest quality oil obtained from the first cold pressing.

Olive oil: is a blend of refined olive oils (obtained from the second pressing) combined with virgin olive oil.

Peanut: made from ground peanuts, is the most commonly-used oil in Asian cooking; however, a lighter type of oil can be used.

Sesame: an oil made from roasted, crushed white sesame seeds. Do not use for frying.

Virgin olive oil: is high quality oil obtained from the first cold pressing.

OLIVE PASTE: made from olives, olive oil, salt, vinegar and herbs.

PARSLEY, FLAT-LEAFED: also known as continental or Italian parsley.

PAWPAW: yellow tropical fruit of the papaya family. The papaya, smaller with deep pink flesh, can be substituted.

PASTRAMI: highly seasoned smoked beef ready to eat when bought.

PEPITAS: dried pumpkin seeds.

PEPPERS: capsicum or bell peppers.

PIMIENTOS: canned or bottled peppers.

PINE NUTS: small, cream-coloured, soft kernels.

PISTACHIO NUTS: to peel skin from pistachio nuts, soak in boiling water for about

5 minutes; drain and then pat dry with absorbent paper. Rub skin away from nut.

PLUM SAUCE: a dipping sauce made of plums, sugar, chillies and spices.

PRAWNS: shrimp.

PROSCIUTTO: uncooked, unsmoked ham cured in salt; ready to eat when bought.

PRUNES: whole dried plums.

REDCURRANT JELLY: a preserve made from redcurrants.

RIND: zest, the coloured part of citrus skin containing flavouring oils.

ROCKET: a green salad leaf.

RUM, DARK: we prefer to use an underproof rum (not overproof) for a more subtle flavour.

SAFFRON: available in strands or ground form. The quality varies greatly.

SAKE: Japanese rice wine. If unavailable, dry sherry, vermouth or brandy can be used.

SAMBAL OELEK (also ulek or olek): made from ground chillies, spices, salt and vinegar.

SCALLOPS: we use the scallops with coral (roe) attached.

SEASONED PEPPER: a combination of peppers, garlic flakes and paprika.

SHRIMP PASTE: also known as prawn paste; is a powerful flavouring made from salted dried shrimp.

SIRLOIN: good-quality beef steak with T-bone or boneless; New York-style steak.

SNOW PEAS: also known as mange tout (eat all).

SNOW PEA SPROUTS: sprouted seeds of the snow pea.

STAR ANISE: the dried star-shaped fruit of an evergreen tree. It has an aniseed flavour and is used sparingly in Chinese cooking.

STOCK POWDER: 1 cup (250ml) stock is the equivalent of 1 cup (250ml) water plus

1 crumbled stock cube (or 1 teaspoon stock powder). If you prefer to make your own stock, see recipes below.

SUGAR: we use coarse granulated table sugar, also known as crystal sugar, unless otherwise specified.

Brown: a soft, fine, granulated sugar containing molasses.

SWEET CHILLI SAUCE: a sauce made from red chillies, sugar, garlic, salt and vinegar.

SWEETENED CONDENSED MILK: we used Nestle's brand which had 60 per cent of water removed, then sweetened with sugar.

SZECHWAN PEPPER: (also known as Chinese pepper). Small red-brown aromatic seeds resembling black peppercorns. They have a peppery-lemon flavour.

TABASCO SAUCE: made with vinegar, hot red peppers and salt. Use in drops.

TAHINI PASTE: made from crushed sesame seeds.

TAMARILLO: oval fruit with burgundy or yellow skin; has red flesh and tangy seeds.

TAMARIND SAUCE: available from Asian food stores. To make a substitute: soak about 30g dried tamarind in a cup of hot water, stand 10 minutes, cool, squeeze pulp as dry as possible and use the flavoured water.

TANDOORI PASTE: Indian blend of hot and fragrant spices including turmeric, paprika, chilli powder, saffron, cardamom and garam masala.

TERIYAKI MARINADE: a blend of soy sauce, wine, vinegar and spices.

TERIYAKI SAUCE: based on the lighter Japanese soy sauce; contains sugar, spices and vinegar.

TIA MARIA: a coffee-flavoured liqueur.

TOMATILLOS: ripe, small, green tomatoes, available in cans.

TOMATO:

Canned: whole peeled tomatoes in natural juices.

Paste: a concentrated tomato puree used in flavouring soups, stews, sauces and casseroles, etc.

Puree: canned pureed tomatoes (not tomato paste). Use fresh, peeled, pureed tomatoes as a substitute, if preferred.

Sauce: tomato ketchup.

Sun-dried: dried tomatoes. We use sun-dried tomatoes bottled in oil unless otherwise specified.

Supreme: a canned product consisting of tomatoes, onions, celery, peppers and seasonings.

VANILLA BEAN: dried bean of the vanilla orchid. It can be used repeatedly; simply wash in warm water after use, dry well and store in an airtight container.

VINEGAR:

Balsamic: originated in the province of Modena, Italy.

Brown: malt vinegar, brewed from malt and fermented spirit.

Cider: made from apples, has an acidic taste.

Rice: a colourless seasoned vinegar containing sugar and salt.

Rice wine: golden in colour and low in alcohol; it is made from fermented rice.

Tarragon: white wine vinegar infused with fresh tarragon.

White: made from spirit of cane sugar.

WHITE FISH: means non-oily fish. This category includes bream, flathead, whiting, snapper, jewfish and ling. Redfish also comes into this category.

WORCESTERSHIRE SAUCE: spicy sauce used mainly on red meat.

MAKE YOUR OWN STOCK

BEEF STOCK
2kg meaty beef bones
2 medium (300g) onions
2 sticks celery, chopped
2 medium (250g) carrots, chopped
3 bay leaves
2 teaspoons black peppercorns
5 litres (20 cups) water
3 litres (12 cups) water, extra

Place bones and unpeeled chopped onions in baking dish. Bake in hot oven about 1 hour or until bones and onions are well browned. Transfer bones and onions to large pan, add celery, carrots, bay leaves, peppercorns and water, simmer, uncovered, 3 hours. Add extra water, simmer, uncovered, further 1 hour; strain.
Makes about 2.5 litres (10 cups).
- Stock can be made 4 days ahead.
- Storage: Covered, in refrigerator.
- Freeze: Suitable.
- Microwave: Not suitable.

CHICKEN STOCK
2kg chicken bones
2 medium (300g) onions, chopped
2 sticks celery, chopped
2 medium (250g) carrots, chopped
3 bay leaves
2 teaspoons black peppercorns
5 litres (20 cups) water

Combine all ingredients in large pan, simmer, uncovered, 2 hours; strain.
Makes about 2.5 litres (10 cups).
- Stock can be made 4 days ahead.
- Storage: Covered, in refrigerator.
- Freeze: Suitable.
- Microwave: Not suitable.

FISH STOCK
1.5kg fish bones
3 litres (12 cups) water
1 medium (150g) onion, chopped
2 sticks celery, chopped
2 bay leaves
1 teaspoon black peppercorns

Combine all ingredients in large pan, simmer, uncovered, 20 minutes; strain.
Makes about 2.5 litres (10 cups).
- Stock can be made 4 days ahead.
- Storage: Covered, in refrigerator.
- Freeze: Suitable.
- Microwave: Not suitable.

VEGETABLE STOCK
1 large (180g) carrot, chopped
1 large (350g) parsnip, chopped
2 medium (300g) onions, chopped
6 sticks celery, chopped
4 bay leaves
2 teaspoons black peppercorns
3 litres (12 cups) water

Combine all ingredients in large pan, simmer, uncovered, 1½ hours; strain.
Makes about 1.25 litres (5 cups).
- Stock can be made 4 days ahead.
- Storage: Covered, in refrigerator.
- Freeze: Suitable.
- Microwave: Suitable.

Index

QUICK CONVERSION GUIDE

Wherever you live in the world you can use our recipes with the help of our easy-to-follow conversions for all your cooking needs. These conversions are approximate only. The difference between the exact and approximate conversions of liquid and dry measures amounts to only a teaspoon or two, and will not make any difference to your cooking results.

MEASURING EQUIPMENT

The difference between measuring cups internationally is minimal within 2 or 3 teaspoons' difference. (For the record, 1 Australian metric measuring cup will hold approximately 250ml.) The most accurate way of measuring dry ingredients is to weigh them. When measuring liquids use a clear glass or plastic jug with metric markings.

If you would like the measuring cups and spoons as used in our Test Kitchen, turn to page 128 for details and order coupon. In this book we use metric measuring cups and spoons approved by Standards Australia.

● a graduated set of four cups for measuring dry ingredients; the sizes are marked on the cups.
● a graduated set of four spoons for measuring dry and liquid ingredients; the amounts are marked on the spoons.
● 1 TEASPOON: 5ml.
● 1 TABLESPOON: 20ml.

NOTE: NZ, CANADA, USA AND UK ALL USE 15ml TABLESPOONS.
ALL CUP AND SPOON MEASUREMENTS ARE LEVEL.

DRY MEASURES

METRIC	IMPERIAL
15g	½oz
30g	1oz
60g	2oz
90g	3oz
125g	4oz (¼lb)
155g	5oz
185g	6oz
220g	7oz
250g	8oz (½lb)
280g	9oz
315g	10oz
345g	11oz
375g	12oz (¾lb)
410g	13oz
440g	14oz
470g	15oz
500g	16oz (1lb)
750g	24oz (1½lb)
1kg	32oz (2lb)

LIQUID MEASURES

METRIC	IMPERIAL
30ml	1 fluid oz
60ml	2 fluid oz
100ml	3 fluid oz
125ml	4 fluid oz
150ml	5 fluid oz (¼ pint/1 gill)
190ml	6 fluid oz
250ml	8 fluid oz
300ml	10 fluid oz (½ pint)
500ml	16 fluid oz
600ml	20 fluid oz (1 pint)
1000ml (1 litre)	1¾ pints

WE USE LARGE EGGS WITH AN AVERAGE WEIGHT OF 60g

HELPFUL MEASURES

METRIC	IMPERIAL
3mm	⅛in
6mm	¼in
1cm	½in
2cm	¾in
2.5cm	1in
5cm	2in
6cm	2½in
8cm	3in
10cm	4in
13cm	5in
15cm	6in
18cm	7in
20cm	8in
23cm	9in
25cm	10in
28cm	11in
30cm	12in (1ft)

HOW TO MEASURE

When using the graduated metric measuring cups, it is important to shake the dry ingredients loosely into the required cup. Do not tap the cup on the bench, or pack the ingredients into the cup unless otherwise directed. Level top of cup with knife. When using graduated metric measuring spoons, level top of spoon with knife. When measuring liquids in the jug, place jug on flat surface, check for accuracy at eye level.

OVEN TEMPERATURES

These oven temperatures are only a guide; we've given you the lower degree of heat. Always check the manufacturer's manual.

	C˚ (Celsius)	F˚ (Fahrenheit)	Gas Mark
Very slow	120	250	1
Slow	150	300	2
Moderately slow	160	325	3
Moderate	180	350	4
Moderately hot	190	375	5
Hot	200	400	6
Very hot	230	450	7

TWO GREAT OFFERS FROM THE AWW HOME LIBRARY

Here's the perfect way to keep your Home Library books in order, clean and within easy reach. More than a dozen books fit into this smart silver grey vinyl folder. PRICE: Australia $9.95; elsewhere $19.95; prices include postage and handling. To order your holder, see the details below.

All recipes in the AWW Home Library are created using Australia's unique system of metric cups and spoons. While it is relatively easy for overseas readers to make any minor conversions required, it is easier still to own this durable set of Australian cups and spoons (photographed). PRICE : Australia: $5.95; New Zealand: $A8.00; elsewhere: $A9.95; prices include postage & handling.
This offer is available in all countries.

TO ORDER YOUR METRIC MEASURING SET OR BOOK HOLDER:

PHONE: Have your credit card details ready. **Sydney:** (02) 260 0035; **elsewhere in Australia:** 008 252 515 (free call, Mon-Fri, 9am-5pm) or *FAX* your order to (02) 267 4363 or *MAIL* your order by photocopying or cutting out and completing the coupon below.

PAYMENT: **Australian residents:** We accept the credit cards listed, money orders and cheques. **Overseas residents:** We accept the credit cards listed, drafts in $A drawn on an Australian bank, also English, New Zealand and U.S. cheques in the currency of the country of issue.
Credit card charges are at the exchange rate current at the time of payment.

Please photocopy and complete coupon and fax or send to:
AWW Home Library Reader Offer, ACP Direct, PO Box 7036, Sydney 2001.

❏ Metric Measuring Set   ❏ Holder

Please indicate number(s) required.

Mr/Mrs/Ms _____

Address _____

_____

Postcode _____ Country _____

Ph: (   ) _____ Bus. Hour: _____

I enclose my cheque/money order for $ _____ payable to ACP Direct

OR: please charge my:

❏ Bankcard ❏ Visa ❏ MasterCard ❏ Diners Club ❏ Amex

☐☐☐☐☐☐☐☐☐☐☐☐☐☐☐☐ Exp. Date ___/__

Cardholder's signature _____

(Please allow up to 30 days for delivery within Australia. Allow up to 6 weeks for overseas deliveries.)

AWSF95